GIVING BACK!

SECOND EDITION

GIVING BACK!

LIFE AND LEADERSHIP FROM THE FARM TO THE COMBAT ZONE AND BEYOND

Dave Nordel, CMSgt, USAF (Ret.)
with Darla Tyler-McSherry

Giving Back!: Life and Leadership from the Farm to the Combat Zone and Beyond
Published by Max Fab Consulting
Billings, Montana, U.S.A.

Copyright Second Edition ©2023, DAVE NORDEL. All rights reserved.

First Edition June 2022

No part of this book may be reproduced in any form or by any mechanical means, including information storage and retrieval systems without permission in writing from the publisher/author, except by a reviewer who may quote passages in a review. All images, logos, quotes, and trademarks included in this book are subject to use according to trademark and copyright laws of the United States of America.

NORDEL, DAVE, Author
GIVING BACK!!
DAVE NORDEL with Darla Tyler-McSherry

Library of Congress Control Number: 2023906814

ISBN: 979-8-9880174-0-0 (paperback)
ISBN: 979-8-9880174-3-1 (paperback)
ISBN: 979-8-9880174-1-7 (hardcover)
ISBN: 979-8-9880174-2-4 (digital)

BUSINESS & ECONOMICS / Leadership
BIOGRAPHY & AUTOBIOGRAPHY / Military
PSYCHOLOGY / Mental Health

Rogue Publishing Partners: (roguepublishingpartners.com):
Editing and Cover Design: Chris O'Byrne (jetlaunch.net)
Interior Design and eBook: Michelle M. White (mmwbooks.com)
Publishing Management and Consulting: Susie Schaefer (finishthebookpublishing.com)

QUANTITY PURCHASES:

Schools, companies, professional groups, clubs, and other organizations may qualify for special terms when ordering quantities of this title. For information, email info@maxfabconsulting.com

All rights reserved by DAVE NORDEL and MAX FAB CONSULTING.

This book is printed in the United States of America.

Ready for a Convoy in Somalia

*To all those true friends and loved ones
who have given me the gifts I can now give back.
(You know who you are.)*

Gramps and his precious cows

Leaders can't self-appoint or anoint.
That only comes from peers and followers.

Contents

Preface 1

Introduction 3

Family Matters 7

Trust Your Instincts—or You Will Get Run Over 10

Nature's Way 13

Keep Looking for Opportunities 16

When You Hear Crying, You Are Close to Making a Change 19

True Friends—Are You a Good One? 22

Listen on a 3x5 Notecard 27

Crying is Not a Sign of Weakness 30

Everyone Has Something to Offer 33

If it Ain't Broke, Don't Fix It 35

Nobody Cares How Much You Know 37

Don't Be a Sheeple 40

Don't Waste Your Time Wondering 43

Use the Right Tools 46

Your Handshake Matters 49

Do Not Underestimate People 51

Are Leaders Born that Way? 54

Aspire, Don't Desire 58

Make the Tough Call	62
A War Story from Iraq	67
Appetites Can Kill You	72
Attitude and Max Fab	78
Don't Take Yourself Too Seriously	81
Teach to Learn, Learn to Teach	84
Every Day is Sunday	88
Slow Down to Go Faster	91
Kids Know Everything	96
When You Can't Milk the Cows Anymore	102
A Note from the Author	107
Acknowledgments	111
Contributions from Darla Tyler-McSherry	113
About the Author	115
An Excerpt from *When the Cows Lie Down*	117

Preface

Giving Back! was inspired by those who saw value in my experiences and encouraged me to write and share my thoughts on life and leadership as experienced and shaped by exceptional people who imparted their gifts to me and help me fill my treasure chest of nuggets I now share with you.

The memoir will take you through experiences early in my life and how they instilled values and lessons in me that helped me navigate through difficult times and successful moments. You will find yourself on the farm and in a combat zone, in near-death situations and interesting environments as you get to see the moments in time that shape the lessons learned at the end of each chapter.

Giving Back! will drive your introspection and reflection, and you will hopefully recall similar situations in your life that can help you navigate the newest challenges you face. Giving Back! is to be shared with those you love and feel may benefit from even the smallest insight. Enjoy the read!

Introduction

The Farm where we all grew up in Orland, California

Attention: This book is not written at a PhD level. Why is that important? In a time where we are all saturated with data, studies, and statistics that drive our lives, I give you an experience devoid of all this. My book has no data or subject matter expert or graph or study or statistical analysis. These are real-life stories and real-life lessons from me, a kid who grew up in a farming community and worked in a combat zone. It's all interrelated to life's lessons. They may not all apply to you, but I hope this prompts you to be introspective and maybe, just maybe, get better in some small way as you travel your path in life!

Now that we made it this far (which makes me happy), let's have some fun. Stay with me! The ride of life is fun and can be all over the place at times, and we only want it to culminate in goodness.

As I have lived my life, I have learned a few things that people close to me felt I should share. I hope you get a peek into my experiences from my earliest memories to across a military career and beyond. Please feel free to take a nugget or two and apply it in a way that will change your life or someone else's in a way that makes a positive difference.

I'll guess and say something must have caught your eye from the book title or a photo. Maybe you think I have some new, deep insight, and I know something you don't. Don't stop here. You know everything in this book's lessons, but are you applying it, thinking about it, or even aware you have blind spots? Many things have happened to me in my time on earth, and I have been asked to speak and mentor about my experiences—which leads people to say, "Why don't you write this down, Dave?" Well, here goes! Get ready to live a little of it with me. Hopefully you'll pause and think, and hopefully it helps you or a loved one or someone you are responsible to lead to take a little easier or more direct path to a better self and a better life and help you be anointed or appointed as a leader by your followers.

I have been pressured (in a loving way) by a few friends to write down my thoughts, and because of them, I chose to share some experiences in my life. This will be the first time my kids hear or read about them or that friends and family will know of my experiences. With that, I appreciate each of you for stretching me in life and keeping me young.

When people ask for my advice on life or leadership, I always say, "Everything you need to know is on the farm or in a combat zone."

I was born to an agricultural family, Portuguese immigrants from four generations prior who I like to call "seasick." (I get violently seasick, and the East Coast Portuguese fishermen have my respect.) They all came to America, and my maternal side settled in the far north of California on the Humboldt coast and became dairy farmers, not fishermen. (Portuguese are good at both.)

After WWII, my grandfather moved his farm along with his brothers to the north of the Sacramento valley in Orland, California. There, they expanded their farming and continued to raise their families. This is the place I would grow up, not only physically, but also morally, socially, and emotionally.

My mother moved from the farm in her younger years and later met my father while working in Sacramento. This relationship shaped me in many ways. My father left for good when I was two and has never been a part of my life to this day.

The tragedy that was my mother's one and only true relationship led us back to the farm, living with or near my grandparents on the farm and doing all the things young children and men do in a country farm environment. I left home at nineteen and never looked back. The lessons learned on the farm and from everything in and on it (animals, work, people) would shape my life in a way that led to a blessed thirty-year military career and a rise in Air Force leadership founded and based on lessons of the farm that served me well in combat areas of operation and all levels of leadership. I had the privilege to serve all over the world and be part of the lives of people and cultures in the most amazing and trying ways imaginable. It was all a blessing and a schoolhouse of endless lessons.

I take you to personal places that are difficult to share and share my stories and the lessons that come with each. I am sure you will find some corollaries that apply to your life, work, and relationships, and I hope I can pass along something that helps you reach your goals and have a happy and balanced life.

Life is not easy, and it's a glorious treasure. You'll see from my life that the most impactful people were not necessarily the best of people or set the best examples. I didn't necessarily like them, nor did they all do right by me.

I purposely chose to not give hard timelines and names of family and friends and people who made it into this writing. If you are in the book, you will know, and I have tried to be as factual as possible. These are my memories (not over-embellished) written in the way I best recall. Please enjoy these times with me as I get my opportunity to *give back!*

It all starts on the farm for me, and this is my journey.

Family Matters

Cousins are the best

When you are the product of Portuguese heritage and culture, family matters. Boy, does family matter!

We learn a lot from cousins, siblings, parents, uncles, aunts, and extended family. Mine was huge. We joked that in my small town of Orland, California, you would have to tell your mom if you wanted to date someone to make sure they weren't a third cousin once removed.

Farms run on hard work, and that work is most likely carried out by family. My experiences had a lot of families on many farms making it happen every day, but there was more to work than making the farm go. You see, you can have many families—your blood family, your work family, or as in my case, a huge, extended military family. All of these require nurturing, patience, and understanding.

As on the farm or in the military or work family, you may be the leader. Families rally in times of need, they celebrate together, and they pull together when people are down, mentally, physically, or even help with a few bucks here and there.

The United States military has its faults, as we all do, but they have no better sense of what I describe as "family." I once saw a wounded brother whisked off the battlefield to our trauma center, and in the middle of the Iraq war, we found a way to bring his other brother from a different part of Iraq to be by his side if even only for just a few moments.

When my grandmother died, the Air Force had me in my mother's house within a day—all the way from Japan. When it was time to retire and hang it up, people came from all over to celebrate my career and help me transition. (It is like a wedding and funeral together.) My military and work families were there, and a dear friend I grew up with came to be at my side, and my father's brother and his son and their wives also made it to the event. These are very important things in one's life.

I have always tried to be there for my families whenever asked, and I take it very seriously. When my phone rang or email pinged, I did my best to answer the call. I feel that those moments are defining in your life and their presence (or absence) is remembered and defined.

One of these sentinel moments came when my mother could not physically take care of herself, and we had to move her to assisted living. Remember: I am her only child, so moving and selling a house, getting her settled, and changing finances was difficult. I had a very special cousin come to my rescue and rally for me, and that will always mean the world to me, more than she will ever know. There were a few who called, mainly to ask for material things or something of mom's that was a memory. There was not a lot of help from most, but my one cousin was right there, the epitome of what "family matters" means.

The ultimate in family matters is your own (my own). As you see throughout this book, I pull from people and times in my life that provided me with great lessons and tools to help navigate this wonderful world we live in.

I want to also stress that I have learned from many sources. Not all are older than me or have some big fancy title. I have learned more from my boys (two of them) and surely my wife (she is my second wife—and boy, did I learn a lot from the first one) of almost thirty years. First and foremost, in "family matters," my boys and wife taught me that it is not about you. That was ingrained in me when our oldest was born and as we made decisions about where to go, what to do, and how to do it, all while we navigated all the things we do in life. You'll see it throughout the book, and you will feel the influence of these three special people in my life. During success and failure, good and bad, they are the constant, and I could not be as far along in life as I am without them. It is terminal love—and with that, family matters!

LESSONS FROM FAMILY MATTERS

- Answer that higher calling. Be there through thick and thin—it will let you sleep better at night.
- In the end, your families will be all you have. Nurture that relationship; it is fragile. Create an environment that embodies family. It will pay off for you as a boss, friend, and family member.
- Pay it forward and trust it will come back to you.
- Families have leaders. Have you been anointed or appointed by yours?
- Find terminal love, and nurture it.

Trust Your Instincts—or You Will Get Run Over

Me on the tractor that didn't run me over

Born in July 1965, I was pretty normal, with ten toes, ten fingers, and a lot of hair. I have no memories of much until one moment when I was about four years old. This was the start of many brilliant and wonderful and not so good farm memories. I always smile when somebody asks what the first thing is I remember. It makes me perk up, and I say, "When I was run over by a tractor!"

On the farm, kids are always out and about and curious as any child. This is in the middle of the normal routine and meeting the basic needs of the animals and the property and the crops. Milking, plowing, milking, planting, milking, fixing a fence, milking, feeding cows—did I mention milking? On this day, it was time to feed the cows, a blah rainy day. In this part of California, rain can be torrential, and this probably saved my life. My uncle was out feeding the cows and that involved a tractor pulling a wagon slowly past the pens and letting the feed come out of the trailer by a conveyor. (Riding the tractor was fun!) This scene was a daily constant, the smell of fresh-cut hay mixed with all the aromas the farm brings. When it rains this way, you can smell the earth as the tractor tires turn up mud and dust. And manure—some call it gross, and some call it the smell of money. It made me appreciate smells, and smells would come back to haunt me later in life.

As we were doing this, the tractor hit a small hole, and off the tractor I went—straight under the back wheel of the tractor and the front of the wagon. I was lucky the ground was wet and had a lot of give under me. This is where the many lessons of the farm begin.

As I started to lead airmen through my career, I quickly referenced this moment in life to ground me when enthusiasm needed to be tempered or we had to slow down to go faster.

Sometime in my thirties, I told my uncle I finally forgave him for running me over. It drew a great big roar from the room. Rest in peace, dear uncle.

The tractor running over me taught me some things that benefitted me while leading airmen and raising a family.

LESSONS FROM TRUST YOUR INSTINCTS

- Be aware of risk. If it looks unsafe, it probably is.
- Trust your gut. You see, my mother said my uncle looked like he was going to die when he carried me in the house, and I looked just fine (after one of only five trips to the doctor in my life), but the rules quickly changed on tractor rides, and a hole or two probably got fixed.
- If it feels unsafe, it probably is.
- If it feels wrong, it probably is. Beware.

- If you are not 100 percent comfy in a situation, then be on guard.
- Who is next to get run over? You better find out sooner than later and fix the holes beforehand.

This is not to say don't take chances, but prepare, train, learn, listen, and plan in a way that gives you the best possibility to succeed in all you do. There are no shortcuts to a tractor ride; either it is safe, or you don't get to ride on the tractor.

Nature's Way

Holstein calves

When I joined the Air Force, I wanted to be a plumber. But they had another idea for me, and they made me a medic. I had no idea that my life would soon be filled with opportunities to help and heal people and be a part of people's lives at the very beginning and there to hold a head or a hand at their end. I did this my entire career and continue today.

The farm teaches some hard lessons that you have to quickly adapt to and understand. The farm is a daily science lab in society, in nature's way. I will never be accused of being patient (I work on this daily) or at times tolerant of people's methods of getting things done. I am a vision guy and can see where we need to be. Well, others don't move fast enough for me at times, although that's not their fault.

I learned how to become better at this, though still far from perfect, by remembering nature's way. On days when I had the whole farm to myself, I'd sit and watch the animals. Some had names, some were identified by their mannerisms, and some by their timeline to go to the auction or the butcher. But on some long hot summer days—these days involve making friends with flies; they are all around and relentless—the cows' tails never stop swishing from side to side, and your hands are never still as you move one fly from a spot only to land on another. The smell of silage and cow shit and urine is thick and all consuming.

I'd sit with my feet swinging over one spot on the cement wall of the manger to watch the cows have their calves. It would start with their water sack starting to hang out of them. At that point, you knew the day had come—but when? Watching this from start to finish is not for someone who is impatient like me, but it sure is a lesson in nature's way. Every cow is different, just as we all are. Every birth is different, every newborn is special, and the outcome is always different, sometimes in big ways or subtle ways, but the one constant is that it is nature's way.

During the long summer days—as hot as 112—I saw calves being born. I saw them born in dirt, in ponds, in places that would cost them their young lives, backward, or having to be sacrificed for the life of their mothers. This was sad. It took patience to observe or intervene, but it was always nature's way.

My first job in the United States Air Force was delivering babies. When asked if I had seen anything like that before or if the blood might bother me, I chuckled and said, "I think I got this one." It is just nature's way. During that blessed year of OB/GYN, I experienced it all, from many special highs with new families, to the most devastating moments of a stillbirth or worse. It was nature that prepared me for that and many more challenges to come.

LESSONS FROM NATURE'S WAY

- If during the worst moments you understand it's nature's way, it helps you get through it.
- Understand your environment and adapt to it.
- Understand that even your best efforts may not change nature's way.
- Nature's way is okay; don't lose sleep over it.
- If you are inpatient, nature can help you cure yourself.

Keep Looking for Opportunities

The only medicine man within miles;
doing humanitarian work in a remote Turkish Village

I know it is cliché to say if you get knocked down, get back up and keep trying, but it is never truer than on the farm and in a small rural town. A story comes to mind that is difficult and not joyful to relive. I was a baseball player, loved the game, studied it, and was actually blessed with a bit of talent hitting and fielding. However, I can't run—at least not very fast. In Orland, I was one of the better players, made all the all-star teams in Little League, and had some good memories. But as I got older and started to mix with other ages and into high school, my weaknesses appeared, and yes, believe it or not, there are politics in baseball. I played on every team, started, and was very productive.

Then came my junior year in high school. Varsity baseball was big-time competition. I showed up and practiced and played my butt off, and then one day the coach said, "Cuts are tomorrow." Cuts had never crossed my mind. Surely, I had done enough, right? When I looked at the cut sheet and saw my name wasn't on there, I had a moment of rejection and loss I had not felt since maybe losing a pet. I was devastated. I ran to my locker, grabbed my stuff, went to the coach's classroom, and literally yelled at him for cutting me and left school. You see, I had placed all my marbles on baseball. What was I going to do for the rest of the year? Who would I hang out with? All my friends had made the team; they would be busy with baseball and hanging out together. Well, as young men do, I drifted to a new set of friends and started doing other things with my spare time. You can guess that some of it wasn't good.

One afternoon, after hanging with a new friend, we were near the ballpark when the team was practicing. I had burned some bridges with those guys and the coach and felt regret and scolded myself for giving up and not doing something to get better. I had stopped looking for opportunities and let myself be defined by this one setback or failure. It was a time for me to reflect on how to best handle it. You see, on the farm you will inevitably forget to turn off irrigation water and flood something, or get a tractor stuck, break something, or cut yourself—all setbacks, all good reasons to quit. If every farmer quit in a drought year, things would be a lot different. You have to find a way.

My way presented itself one day in the oddest fashion. A couple of the star players on the team got caught drinking. It was a school issue, and the penalty was removal from the team. When I first heard this, I said it served them right; they cut me, and this was their penalty. But I soon realized it might be an opportunity. I had to swallow my pride, be humble, and hope I had not damaged things to a point that I couldn't get back on the team. After a couple of days, I found the coach and said, "Coach, if you have two empty slots, why can't I fill one for the rest of the year?"

Coach was tough. He later got a World Series ring as a scout during the Mets 1986 championship. I didn't know how he would respond; it was scary and vulnerable, but I needed to take a chance. Well, Coach did what good leaders, coaches, and teachers do. Not only did he take me back, but he also gave me a few opportunities during the rest of that year. And the next year, we worked hard. I was all-league, had one of the highest batting averages in school history, and played in the finals for the section championships.

LESSONS FROM LOOKING FOR OPPORTUNITIES

- Put your marbles in a few spots. Don't lose them all if your plan doesn't work out.
- Adversity builds you and creates opportunity. Don't let it steer you into poor choices.
- Always keep looking for opportunity and have the courage to ask and not wonder about things. Be vulnerable.
- Maintain relationships. People who work for you today may be your bosses later in life.
- We all need coaches, teachers, and mentors. These are people who don't always tell you what you want to hear, but what you need to hear. They are treasures. Treat them that way, and don't run away when it is hard.
- When you put up a new fence and the cows push it over, build a better fence. Don't give up.

When you have a "drought" in your life, hopefully you have planned for it and become resourceful and can work through it. It will make you tougher—and the rains will come soon. *Do not quit!*

When You Hear Crying, You Are Close to Making a Change

In the middle of nowhere, Somalia

I was sitting with my Air Force boss at the time, a two-star general, and he had just instituted a change throughout the entire Intercontinental Ballistic Missile force for our country. Nuclear decisions are important. On this day, he was frustrated. Almost all of his senior officers and my senior enlisted airmen were kicking and screaming about the new way of doing things and how (insert your word here) it all was. As I saw his frustrations, my mind went straight to the farm. Change requires living with the crying and screaming. I asked the general if he had ever been on a farm. He said no, and I decided to share this phenomenon on the farm.

When the cows have calves, the young get to spend a couple of days with Mom. Then, Mom needs to start cycling back to the milk barn, and the calves get put on bottled feedings; this is called weaning. This is a fun time for a kid on the farm; feeding babies is cool. However, there has to be change. Soon these babies need to be weaned off milk and put on feed (grains or hay). This process is done by stopping their milk (changing their environment and routine) and offering grain.

What happens next can make for a long two or three weeks. The calves, once taken off milk, start to cry. They cry all day and all night, and it can keep you awake at times. This can be likened to playing the same song over and over again or the tactic of torture when using noise to manipulate people's psyche. It really makes you want to give them the milk. They get grain every day and plenty of water but no milk. All they know is that they are in the midst of change, and initially, they hate it. Miraculously, they eventually stop, they adjust, they eat plenty of grain, get bigger, and become productive to the farm.

When you lead change, how do you manage the crying? This happens in families every day and in our personal lives. What do you do, and how do you do it? It is on the report card you get when being assessed as a leader.

LESSONS FROM MAKING A CHANGE

- Change is constant; get through it and adapt. The amount of "crying" that you do is dependent on you.
- Not all change is good; not all change is bad. However, change is inevitable.
- Be open to change. Cry if you must but understand that it is going to happen.
- Make the choice, "Do I change, or do I change my situation?"

Change drives movement and change in your life will make you move forward, backward, or someplace else. Regardless, it is moving you. Embrace it, look at it as opportunity, cry as little as possible, and move in whichever direction the change takes you.

True Friends—Are You a Good One?

The flag and some of my heroes in Balad, Iraq

When times are great, who are your friends? Better yet, who are your best friends? When times are tough, when what you have to face requires a support system, like cancer, trauma, or maybe your daughter was raped, then who are your friends? Who is there, who is engaged, who can handle you when you are at your worst—and most importantly, who is still there when it is all over. Who magically appears again after the dust settles?

I prompt you with that because drought comes to the farm, bills sometimes go unpaid, or you may hurt your back and can't milk, a twice-a-day chore every single day of the year. What does that look like in your life, and who shows up, stays the course, and asks for nothing in return?

I learned a lot of "friend lessons" in my thirty years of military service. One would think you have many friends—war buddies, guys and gals you were stationed with in a faraway land, and so on. I came away from my time in the Air Force with a very small handful of friends. There are a lot of acquaintances I care about but very few friends. How do I know? Because in the times when I couldn't "milk the cows" or "haul the hay," there have been people who have shown up. They come from odd places: from my childhood (there is one to this day always there for me), my family (the one true friend in the family is related to me only by marriage), and two cousins who I know are always there.

I once got into trouble when in high school. It was nothing to go to jail over, but still it was hard, trying, and embarrassing. High school is a rough place for people to know your business. When it is bad news, kids are brutal. I was in a pretty low spot, and even a coach and teacher or two abandoned me. One day, one of my buddies I grew up with sat down next to me in the gym and said, "Hey, man, are you all right? I'm checking because you are my friend, and we care about you." If I wrote his name here, he would barely remember the moment, if at all. I will never forget it.

On the farm or in life, sometimes your true friends are the neighbor down the road, that coworker you see every day but don't spend a lot of time with, or a cousin or war buddy. Take some time to decide who those people are. Make sure you are a true friend and put yourself in situations where, when you need help, you ask the right people so you get the return on investment that is realized in true friendships and not relationship of convenience during the good or fun times.

A note from a friend:

I met Dave Nordel when our institution participated in an emergency response exercise that he facilitated. The intent of that exercise was for our community to practice responding to a communicable disease outbreak. How fortuitous for us he chose that topic, as just a few short months later, the world experienced the initial outbreak of the ensuing COVID-19 pandemic. What initially stood out to me was Dave's intentional efforts to gather input from all people in the room, and how easily he adapted and pivoted the plan to incorporate all voices. He didn't dig in his heels and act inflexible and rigid with the original plan designs.

The exercise implementation day arrived, and I was one of the several newbies to the event. Mistakes were made that frustrated some of the more experienced people involved. I arrived at the subsequent debriefing meeting with a healthy dose of apprehension and anxiety, as I was embarrassed over my mistakes and felt I had failed in my duties. Dave must have picked up on that, because I remember seeing a look on his face that was part compassion, part concern, and an expression of "What the heck is wrong?" Dave did not deliver an admonishing assessment of the overall outcomes; instead, he acknowledged that it was a first-time experience for many involved, and the point of conducting an exercise is to learn, not to "get it right" the first time.

I so appreciated how he responded in this manner, and by doing so, he forged a path of trust and communication. This path allowed for the development of a colleague and mentor relationship, which has evolved into a close friendship that has had a profound, positive impact on my life. How close? Anyone who knows me well knows the love and devotion I have for my animals. He is the only person on the entire planet who, other than myself, has permission to drop off and pick up my dog from doggie daycare.

Our institution brought Dave on board as our emergency planner to head up our COVID response efforts. He demonstrated that not only does he "talk the talk," but also "walks the walk." He was on campus each day by 0600, talking to custodians, giving a pep talk to the student-athletes on their way to and from early-morning practices, and consulting with campus and community leadership on our response strategies. Dave facilitated the campus COVID Task Force meetings, which brought together a collective of faculty and staff across campus to report on and get advice and strategy for their new, and often unfamiliar, duties in their Incident Command Structure positions.

To this day, I still have colleagues share with me that they miss these meetings. Why? Because they were action-oriented, to the point, inclusive, and transparent. It was also helpful to hear Dave's animated expressions of "You gotta keep it light!" and "Don't drop the baby!", as he reminded us of the importance of keeping balance and perspective. We were building the plane as we were flying it, and Dave's steady, visible leadership, confidence, inclusivity, and sense of humor allowed and fostered an assurance and camaraderie within the team that reinforced the belief that we would successfully get through the pandemic.

Dave willingly shares his learned leadership lessons, 30,000-foot views, and personal insights from his days as a boy and young man on the family California dairy farm and his military career of more than thirty years. He recently told me, "It's not about Dave being right, it's about being willing to listen and consider," when discussing the mentor role he has had with so many fortunate individuals over the years. One especially profound statement he had made: "True leaders understand that knowledge is most powerful when shared." Pretty incredible, right? Dave lives by this belief each and every day.

This book is one example of Dave "giving back." I am thankful for his attitude and actions of sharing and developing others. Because of this, I have a broader perspective, changed how I work with my team, and am a stronger, more confident person who attempts to "keep it light!" Good on you for choosing to read this book. You'll not only learn from him, but you'll also learn a lot about yourself, too.

-Darla Tyler-McSherry

LESSONS FROM TRUE FRIENDS

- If you're a friend, always be there and every time.
- Being a true friend requires work.
- Not everyone has to be your friend. It is okay to just hang out.
- If you have expectations of a friend, let them know; it saves disappointment.

Listen on a 3x5 Notecard

Defense of the ICBMs

The farm is full of sounds; they are constant and normal. If they are absent, something is wrong or needs to be checked on. If they are new or different, the same applies. But on the farm, you listen.

Sounds are great clues to being successful. The noise a tractor makes, the sound of pumps and machinery, and what the animals transmit can stop you in your tracks to investigate and mitigate something bad or discover something new. The small meow behind a pile of hay can mean a neat discovery as to where the barn cat has hidden her kittens. Or maybe it's the sudden extreme mooing that signals a predator in the midst of the livestock. We listen.

One of my supervisors (and a friend), who has been a blessing to me to this day, once had to do something that was painful but necessary. The story goes like this. I was hand selected to go to the Nevada desert to help start up the first Unmanned Aerial Vehicle or

UAV (drones) squadrons for the United States Air Force. As you can imagine, this was a big job and a big honor, and it required a lot of thinking and strategy.

All of us are built differently. There are introverts (not me) and extroverts (definitely me). Some of us are doers and great at certain things; others are more strategic and abstract. We can drive each other crazy unless we listen.

You see, I was on a roll; I had a vision. My boss was there, as was the rest of the team. As usual, I "knew" the way, until one day I was in a meeting, and I was transmitting (I am good at that) and had it all figured out. What I thought was the big win was a total flop and would lead to some rough mentoring. I had made a huge mistake. My tractor engine was making a poor sound, and I didn't hear it. I was so focused on the harvest that I was going to break the equipment to get it done (lose the support of my commanders and leaders). I stopped listening. My boss at the time, in fine military fashion, made damn good and sure my eyes opened back up quick.

To this day, I struggle with slowing down to listen, but I am much better and really work on it. But on that day, after I emotionally recovered from the gift I received from my boss, I took a 3x5 notecard, wrote *Listen* in bold letters, and put that in my pocket. When I had to be in places where that was necessary, I would pull it out to help me stay balanced. That gift, I can assure you, has saved my life. My time in a farming community has saved my life. What you hear can drive how you make decisions, both the split-second ones and the thought-out ones.

Listening is a communication skill we don't often work on, yet it may be the most important. Take time to listen. If you are bad at it, get your version of a 3x5 card and get better. You will love it when you get to be the first one to tell everyone you know where the barn cat has her kittens.

LESSONS FROM *LISTEN*

- Your ideas get better when you hear and listen to other viewpoints.
- Learning can best be accomplished with your mouth shut.
- Explore the sounds in life that don't seem normal. You may save a life.
- Remember to ask questions that drive you to hear and listen and learn.

Crying is Not a Sign of Weakness

A burn pit in Iraq

"Don't cry!" "Well, it frickin' hurts!" This is the way every childhood injury starts. On the farm, you get hurt. In life, you get hurt, and sometimes the scar is just that, healed but always there. But you should never cry, right? (Insert danger sign here.) Horses are romantic, smart, and gorgeous. They are also six to eight feet off the ground, run fast, and don't like having people on their backs or being whipped.

When I was eleven or twelve, my cousins all visited the farm from Reno, Nevada. These were some of the best times I had on the farm. When the cousins came, there was always lots of fun, and boy, did we find stuff to do. One of the magical things was that our parents definitely didn't "helicopter" over us; we did what we wanted.

One day, my cousin decided we were going to ride a horse—bareback. What could go wrong? Well, she decided that I had to get on the horse with her. I wasn't too keen on it, but what the heck, why not? With every other cousin cheering and yelling and thinking this was a good idea, I was boosted on the horse. As I hung on to her waist, she said, "Give me your belt." I should have jumped off, but I coughed up my belt. As you can imagine, she whipped the horse, and off I went, hitting my head on a piece on concrete. Blood was everywhere, not to mention *I cried!*

These frequent trips back into the house when the cousins were there involved a scratch, a sprain, a cut, or in my case, a head injury. So, bleeding, cut, and hurt, I cried in the kitchen while half a roll of paper towels was used to stop the bleeding, all the while being told, "Stop crying!" You see, crying was weakness. The absence of crying showed you were strong and also not hurt anymore. (I am now a registered nurse of the emergency room variety, and I know now this is the wrong way to approach it.)

During my last combat tour, I forgot some of the lessons of the farm, and it scarred me forever. This book is not going to be a war story or some highlight reel of my career, but there were times during my military service when the lessons of the farm collided. This was one of them.

I was the senior leader for all the enlisted men and women of the trauma center for all of Iraq in 2008. During the surge, the place was busy with patients, civilians, routine stuff, and of course, combat wounded and casualties. I chose to work and lead from the front lines with my people. I put scrubs on and went and nursed during these events. It was great for me and the team, and I was comfortable there.

Then, at times, we had killed-in-action casualties, and these were very involved moments. Our trauma bay would be filled with gurneys of deceased soldiers, sailors, Marines, and airmen, their bodies draped in flags, and the entire staff paying tribute to them over a prayer and a call to attention in the trauma bay. We held a hand salute until they were all wheeled out for their journey back to their loved ones.

This was intense and highly emotional. There wasn't a dry eye in the room or the trauma center, except for one guy, the tough guy, the guy who couldn't cry because he would be seen as weak, not able to lead through the next event. I would sometimes lie in bed (five hours max out of my day) with the smell of blood and plastic explosives in my nose and want to cry, but I didn't allow it. I had to make it through this tour without showing that emotion.

This damaged me, and yes, I later cried after getting home, but it was too late. I forgot to remember the lessons from the farm: if it hurts, it's okay to cry. It might speed healing and help make the scar a bit smaller and easier to live with. I'm not saying you should be a "crybaby," but I am saying we have emotions for a reason. The chemicals in our body balance off of them, and it's important not to hold them back in an appropriate manner.

The famous basketball coach Jimmy Valvano, in his speech accepting an ESPY award a few months before he died, said a good day was a day in which you laughed, were brought to great emotion, cried, and took time to think, laugh, cry, and think. That was a good day. His words are wise, and I often watch that video when faced with difficult days. Make sure you have as many Jimmy V days as you need to be happy and healthy.

LESSONS FROM CRYING IS NOT A SIGN OF WEAKNESS

- Being "strong" can actually make you weak.
- No emotion is unhealthy.
- Why are you scared to cry? The answer is your first step to being healthier in life.
- Don't be a crybaby—but cry when you need to. It's okay.

Everyone Has Something to Offer

The brothers and my gramps solving the world's problems

One could argue that to be a "good" farmer, you have to be a good bullshitter. I tend to agree but have no official study or data to support this. What I do have is many experiences of participation and listening to these interactions, and it helped me through my military time and today.

You see, one should bullshit when they are capable of doing two things, telling the truth and actually knowing what they are talking about. I worked in some interesting circles with very bright people and some with incredible educations and in very responsible positions. It always amazes me that some of these people would start off conversations with statements like "What you fail to understand" and in their own way make you feel like you had missed some great data point that made you less informed. In all actuality, what was going on is these people confused position power with knowledge, just like a PhD confuses education with common sense or intelligence versus education.

Where am I going with this? Offering respect and not assuming being comfortable enough to let others contribute can make you better without looking weak or stupid. Letting experts talk about what they know and listening and learning make you stronger, no matter what letters are behind your name or the title of your job. I watched very bright people who didn't own cows act like it, and it was embarrassing to watch.

I live in Montana now, and when I was stationed in Cheyenne, I had cowboy hats for social events, but I don't wear my hats in Montana. You know why? I don't have cattle, and I don't farm anymore. I can talk a bit about my young life on a farm, but I am not current, so I ask a lot of questions. I never want to be that guy they say is all hat and no cattle. Don't be that person in life. People will respect you for letting them be the smartest person in the room. Let them have the spotlight. Don't be afraid of visibly not knowing something; it will actually enrich you, make you more credible, and you'll get a title you can't earn in college or a trade school. That title is "good leader" or even "great leader."

LESSONS FROM EVERYONE HAS SOMETHING TO OFFER

- Get over yourself.
- Listen to learn.
- Learn to listen.
- Respect.
- Park your ego.
- Put your titles in your pocket.
- Don't BS people; they can smell it. It could define you negatively for life.

If it Ain't Broke, Don't Fix It

The UN was a big part of the Somalia mission

The title of this chapter I am sure you have heard once or twice, but boy, have I lived it. The first time I had a brush with fixing the unbroken was when I was five or six. You see, I loved to take things apart but was not so good at reassembly. I took a few things apart that were needed around the farm, and it didn't put me in a favorable situation—in other words, a well-deserved ass-beating.

I once thought the old hay truck was dirty, so I decided to clean her up. This was the most reliable vehicle on the farm. It never went far, always started, and was a key piece of equipment for feeding the animals. But it was dirty, so I washed her up, cleaned the inside out, stored all the tools nicely, and the next day it wouldn't run. The farmer who was renting the land and milked his cows there (an old family friend and exceptional people to and for me) looked at me and said, "If it ain't broke, don't fix it!

In my military days, I had to say that to myself a lot. While leading or following or trying to accomplish the mission, you need to find happiness where you are. Be appreciative of what you have. You don't need to take apart a relationship, a job environment, or a place where you live just because it hasn't changed, or you think you can make it better. If it is working, don't fix it. Take the time to maintain those things that work; nurture all these things and help them grow. There will be enough in life to "fix," I promise you. Keep the things that work healthy so they don't break, but don't always think they can be better. I watched a lot of fellow airmen chase or change something because they thought it would be better when all the things they needed to be successful were already right there.

I once saw an opportunity to go to Butte, Montana, and work at the medical entrance facilities for new recruits. I was in Japan and having one of the most fruitful times in my career, but I just knew the Butte, Montana thing was the right thing to do next. Then one of my chiefs told me, "I think everything you need is right here in front of you, Dave—but if you *really* want to go to Butte...." I listened. I didn't try to change or fix what wasn't broken, and he was right. My career vaulted over the next two years.

LESSONS FROM IF IT AIN'T BROKE, DON'T FIX IT

- Be happy and appreciate all you have.
- Take care of what works. You'll have plenty of things to fix.
- Don't lose sight of what is right in front of you because the grass might be greener right where you are standing.
- If you are going to take it apart, make sure it is broken and you know how it goes back together.

Nobody Cares How Much You Know

Outside the Army Hospital in Mogadishu

As I grew into leadership roles in my Air Force time, I always tried to use the adage that people come first, leaders eat last, and so on. These are clichés but also true. If you live it and walk the walk, they set a good example and build credibility. But what I learned most from the farm and later heard by some smart person I was fortunate enough to meet was about caring. Before I lose some of you who are thinking, *Oh boy, here comes the touchy-feely stuff*, please stick with me.

I always remember learning about milk barn etiquette. You see, cows, like horses, react to people and how they present themselves. When cows are comfy—have a stable environment, feel safe, and have their needs met—they give more milk, digest food better, stay healthy, and don't cause problems. This leads to barn etiquette. We played soft radio and didn't yell or scream or make loud noises.

People not familiar with the barn usually were asked not to stay long or to step out during milkings. This may sound odd, but I saw it many times. Someone comes into the barn and breaks etiquette, and the cows poop everywhere and they act up when milked. It's because they don't trust they are safe and cared for.

As we go through life with friends and family or interacting in a leader role, it is very simple. Nobody cares how much you know until they know how much you care about them. I hear younger people that I mentor say, "They don't care." It always yanks at my gut when I hear this because I know what their problems are. It's hard to help when you are in a situation where someone in the important parts of your life (work, family, health, spirit) demonstrates a lack of caring or doesn't value that part of leadership. It can be devastating. Just like the cows who give milk to the farmer who cares for them, people need the same. When you demonstrate that in life and demand it from those who play a key role in your life, the return on investment is a hundredfold.

Caring can be demonstrated through actions during tough times—recognizing important events, checking in on a sick child or dog, being available and present if there is a need, and filling the need if possible. That means being present physically, emotionally, and, if need be and appropriate, financially. Be consistent in your actions.

A work partner got sick not long ago. I sent her a note that said, "Do you need anything?" I got a shopping list, everything from chocolate to nasal spray, so off I went shopping, dropped it at her front door, and went about my day. I was prepared to shop. If you say it, be prepared to do it. If you truly care, it will come back to you!

LESSONS FROM NOBODY CARES HOW MUCH YOU KNOW

- Be present and consistent.
- Be prepared to go the extra mile.
- Recognize people and be genuine.
- Tell the truth.
- Don't violate safe space, maintain it.
- Nobody cares how much you know until they know how much you care.

Don't Be a Sheeple

Line of sheep

As I mentioned, not everything we learn is from people we respect or bundled in some romantic story of life on a farm. Sometimes the animals teach us behavior which should not be emulated or at least give us pause to see traps we can fall into.

I mentioned that old feed truck earlier. That truck is a prop in a great experiment. You see, animals—cows, sheep, and other livestock—are creatures of habit and routine. They react to sounds and visuals, and they all tend to just follow that routine to a fault. Sound familiar? Alarm at five, start coffee, brush teeth, shower, clothes, second cup of coffee, etc. Routine makes us feel comfy and safe and keeps things uncomplicated. We all know water takes the path of least resistance, and so do we.

It always amazed me that if we used that truck on the farm for anything other than feeding, the cows would follow it for over a mile, even if it didn't have a single bale of hay on it. They were cued on routine habits and what the truck had to offer. Unfortunately, a large portion of our society tends to do the same, and like sheep, they get very upset when that routine is broken.

It saddens me to see this at times, because we miss so much of life and lose opportunities to make a real difference or find that nugget. We also used that truck at times to get the herd to a place we needed them without much effort. Sometimes that was to get them to a loading point and take them to sale or slaughter.

When I retired from the Air Force, my oldest son and I took a trip to Kansas City to see a couple of baseball games. We had a great time, and at that time, I was still drinking. I didn't want to drive, so we took a cab both nights. This was a place I knew, and we had been to games previously, so a routine existed. When the game is over in KC, the taxis line up, and the people line up. Unfortunately, there are always more people than cabs. As we started to get in line, I told my son, "Let's go. We can walk to the top of the hill toward the interstate." We took a well-beaten path taken by many to get to their hotels by the interstate. We took sixty seconds to climb the hill, and on the other side were taxis headed to the ballpark, so we hailed a cab and got in. He drove past the entire line of people, and we went home. I tipped generously, and my son asked, "Shouldn't we have waited in line?"

My reply was, "Son, in life you can be a sheeple, or you can find a way less traveled but adventurous and fruitful, and then you expand and learn. I'd even argue that being a sheeple could put you more at risk than make you safe."

LESSONS FROM DON'T BE A SHEEPLE

- Be yourself.
- Take acceptable risks.
- Find alternate paths.
- Trust your instincts.
- Don't follow the truck to the slaughter.
- Put yourself in situations to learn and grow, even if they scare the poop out of you.

Don't Waste Your Time Wondering

Collaborating with the Commander - airshow day!

This chapter may stray from the farm a bit, but as I reflect on things in my life and my career that were lessons learned, I wish I could easily get people to understand what I mean when I say, "Stop wondering and go find out." Where the farm and my culture play into this is life-defining. I grew up in a white and brown American-Portuguese community, with farming and all that goes with the culture and heritage. I am proud to be Portuguese (100 percent at that). However, the farm and the community come with limitations. We didn't have many people from other races around us. There was one black kid we all grew up with (in my graduating class) who was raised by white parents. Otherwise, we were white or brown (Mexican, Portuguese, and a few others).

Boy, did I have a rude awakening when I went into the Air Force. My basic training flight had a lot of different people, and I was doing a lot of wondering. *What is their story? What is it like to be black or Asian?* And so on. I was selected to be a squad leader, and that made me responsible for twelve or thirteen guys and their activities. I enjoyed the challenge but soon found out that some of the things I brought from the farm were not so "bueno." I found my squad running late one day, and we had to finish making beds. One of the airmen (who was black and from Philadelphia) was having trouble making his corners. I went to help him, and in the middle of it I said just, "Come on, (insert N word), rig it, and let's go." I had no idea what I had just done.

This time in my life turned out to be a blessing on many levels. First, I was there with some pretty sharp black airmen who realized I was an ignorant farm kid and needed to be educated. They took me aside and asked what my problem was. Did I realize what I had said and what that meant in the world they came from? I felt terrible and wanted to evaporate. That term was commonplace where I grew up. Maybe for some it was meant to be racist or derogatory, but mostly it was just ignorance.

Once I realized that I had a gap, I told myself, *As long as you are in this world, don't ever wonder again. Find out, ask questions, try to be empathetic and real. Don't assume anything and check yourself before you end up looking like something less than you are.*

You see, I was given the gift of empathy, understanding, and grace. This one moment in time sent me in a direction that served me well through thirty years in the Air Force and still today. I stopped wondering, tried to walk a mile in shoes I could never completely understand, and got a lot of help when I was out of my league trying to make someone's life better or easier as we all grew together in our careers. I am proud of the fact that I found opportunities for people that they may not have had, based on their race or gender, and I am proud to say that many have far surpassed my accomplishments and are making our world a better place every day.

LESSONS FROM DON'T WASTE YOUR TIME WONDERING

- If you don't know, don't fake it—ask.
- Understand you have gaps. Don't wonder, fill them.
- Empathy is the path to growth. Slow down and learn about people. It only makes you stronger.
- Check yourself. Don't become a fool because you think your way is the only way.
- Expose yourself to situations that are not comfortable.
- Trust, but verify.

Use the Right Tools

Montana has fish!

I am famous for tools. If my family were around, they would quickly tell you about the hammer trees growing on our farm, because as good farm kids, we can grow things. My thing one year was to grow hammer trees, so every hammer on the farm got buried and watered. This caused a small problem when a fence needed mending, and it wasn't as funny as it is now, but it is my legacy, and boy, do I pay for it at times.

The tool of choice on the farm is the pocketknife. We all start carrying one at a young age because you need one—a lot. It is not always the right tool, but because it is right there in your pocket and doesn't require a walk to the barn or shop, you use the knife for a job it isn't intended for. Those who know what I am talking about have at least one scar on their hand from doing this. Ironically, once you cut yourself, you walk to the shop, get the right tool, and fix what you are working on.

We have lots of tools in our lives. They come in the form of phones, computers, social workers, and books. Heck, we even have Google. During my time in the Air Force, managing and leading, I found that a lot of people picked the wrong tools. Some of these led to tragedy that to this day burns a hole in my soul. In life, we struggle, things break, and we need tools to fix them. They are all right there. Some require effort, some require us to check our ego, and others require us to be completely vulnerable. You have to take the long walk to the shop to get what you need.

I worked for one colonel who got frustrated because we needed a certain special skillset to accomplish a mission we had in our clinic. He said to me, "Chief, when I'm trying to make bread, why do they keep sending me candlestick makers and not bakers?" That has stuck with me for a long time as I try to mentor people not to settle for a pocketknife because it is expeditious but to find the right tool.

The tragedies I mention above are suicides. You see, most, if not all of those people, had access to what they needed, tools to help them with what was broken. However, in the end, they either had too much pride, too little self-esteem, or a general lack of knowledge of what would have been better choices to help deal with it all.

One day in Iraq, we had three soldiers kill themselves. All three of them had frontline combat time (two had multiple tours), and all three decided to commit suicide after events they couldn't control. This was not some awful wartime event or something in their military life; it was personal stuff back home and out of their control, and they chose not to use the help that was provided. I dwell on this as I think through using the right tools and finding help.

LESSONS FROM USE THE RIGHT TOOLS

- Find help—it is there.
- Don't self-treat or settle for expediency. Go get the right tools.
- Check your ego and pride. They close avenues to help and access to tools.
- You are valuable and good. Remind yourself of that. What you tell yourself, you listen to. Make it goodness.
- Fill your toolbox in life. Be able to fix your problems.

Your Handshake Matters

Shaking hands with the Secretary of Defense

I remember my grandfather taking my hand and teaching me a genuine handshake (at least in his evaluation). It was a deep-palmed, firm, not obnoxiously hard or strong, confident handshake that wasn't worth anything unless you could look a guy in the eye at the same time and start a relationship right then and there.

"Manners matter," he would say. I was walking into a store with him one day (I was probably six), and I bolted in as he opened the door—only to feel this hand around my arm pulling me off my feet and placing me right back where I started. You see, there was a lady coming into the store; the door had been opened for her. The word "manners" was discussed for a few long minutes. He would be proud today. I open doors for people every day (literally and figuratively), and I enjoy it. It is the right thing to do, and I love doing it.

You get that one chance to make a first impression. You probably don't think about it, but you do. People you don't know gather impressions based on how you are dressed and how you talk, walk, and interact. These moments can be defining when it comes to a time when you need a job, need a hand, or want to influence someone to change. If you are a person charged with the care and feeding of people, or a manager who is required to lead, these moments will be defined by things like your handshake, your eye contact, and your manners and mannerisms.

Get this right. Your reputation is important. Pay attention to feedback, and fight for it. If somebody says you should be doing more or less of something—change a word you use, or dress a bit differently—treat this as a gift.

LESSONS FROM YOUR HANDSHAKE MATTERS

- Work on this daily. Your reputation matters.
- Fight for feedback.
- Embrace the gifts of input and feedback.
- If you manage and are in positions that make you the lead, check yourself and your impressions.
- Everyone is watching all the time. Make them see good or great and someone they want to emulate.

Do Not Underestimate People

All dressed up for the day

When we are younger, we have less of a filter, and kids can be brutal and sometimes mean. Remember when you (or your kids now) said something like "Mommy, that lady is fat," they laughed, and you wished you were under a rock. How would that play out if the "fat" lady walked over and said to your child, "Dear, I was once a model, and when I was thirty-five. I developed cancer, and all the effort it has taken me to stay alive has made me fat, and there is little I can do about that." Would you look at her differently? Would you apologize, empathize, or just say, "I will pray for you?"

In the farming world, the guy or gal who has a ripped flannel shirt, pants tucked in their boots (a Montana thing for sure), and an "Elmer Fudd" hat on looks like someone who is trying to find their next meal. Well, on the farms of Montana, these are the people who have thousands of acres of wheat and large numbers of cattle and are worth millions. They are treasures, they have stories, and they are truly good people.

As we went through numerous conflicts in my thirty years of service, we realized as a nation that we wanted to be thankful for those who were serving, no matter what we were doing. I might part ways with my brothers and sisters in arms here, but like this chapter, we all have a story; there's no right and wrong to it. As I walked through airports and city streets, people bought me drinks and lunches and always said, "Thank you for your service." Initially, that was uplifting, but after a while it became hollow. It almost felt like they were executing a ritual that made them feel better about themselves in some odd way.

I had a cousin who told me, "I always thank people for their service." I told her how I felt about it, and she asked me what I thought she should do.

I told my cousin, "Why don't you ask them what their story is? You see, you may be talking to a brand-new airman who will tell you, 'I have been in a week and haven't been anywhere but joined because my family all served.' It's like asking a rancher how many head of cattle he has, how his farm started, and what kind of cattle he has. My one farmer friend had ninety-nine years of DNA in his herd, three-plus generations. He looks like that guy I described earlier. I would never have known had I not asked."

I used to do a small drill with some airmen. I loved doing it with our Security Forces (Defenders). They spend a lot of hours together on guard posts and in vehicles patrolling, and they consider themselves friends. I would start by telling them some of what is in this chapter and challenge them, "Do you know each other well?" They would always say, "Yes, Chief."

So I would grab one of them and in sixty to ninety seconds, I would ask a series of questions: Where are you from? Do you have a family? What do you do for fun? Have you ever been arrested? Are your parents still married and alive?

Every time, I would look at these men and women and ask, "Who just found out something new?" And all of them would say something like, "I didn't know your dad died, or you like fishing." This exercise is amazing and enables you to make people feel valued and good about themselves. Don't waste the equivalent amount of time it takes you to pour a coffee or make a sandwich and not do this.

We often pass judgments without knowing the story. We don't have time for stories, do we? We have it all figured out. Maybe not so much.

LESSONS FROM DO NOT UNDERESTIMATE PEOPLE

- Assumptions are dangerous and can make you look small and uneducated. Be careful.
- Slow down. Take time to find out someone's story before you call them "fat." This might help you grow.
- Remember: If you make assumptions about others, they are doing the same in return. What do their assumptions say?
- People feel good when you ask them to talk about themselves. Let them do it. It empowers you and them.

Are Leaders Born that Way?

Speech at the VFW

We live in a world of hierarchy. Who is your boss, who is your dad, your mother? There is structure everywhere you turn. When you are unhappy with customer service, you say, "Can I please speak to your supervisor?"

I have heard the question asked, "Are leaders born or are they created?" This is chicken and egg stuff. I do know that some of our greatest leaders were born into similar situations: only children raised only by their mothers seem to have a corollary with other long lineages of families that have produced leaders over generations.

On the farm, it is obvious who the leader is. But who leads in the animal world? Are they born? Are they elected? (In my opinion, leaders are not elected.) Are they a certain species or breed? If you watch cattle coming to the barn or heading to feed, there always seems to be that cow who is always first and leads the way through the field or the mud. Is that cow the leader? Well, the rest certainly follow, but why?

Are you in a position that requires you to lead things? Has someone said you are in a leadership position? Do you say, "I am the leader of…?"

Leaders are individuals who are validated as such by their followers. Leadership is not synonymous with a title, position, or letters behind your name. You may be a manager of human or other resources, but leadership is a tag you are given by the people you are influencing to move a certain direction and how they feel about where you are taking them.

On my last combat tour, I was asked to fill in for our command chief in Iraq. A leadership role, right? Well, the command chief was going on an R & R for just over a month, so I was to fill in. This is a big deal, with lots going on all over Iraq that requires oversight and decision making, so it was a little intimidating. But it was a challenge I was excited to take on—leadership at a new level.

On his way out the door, my friend the command chief said, "Oh, by the way, the vice president will be here next week. You are on the planning team." I laughed and said thanks a bunch. We had a great team, and this went well, but it was a leader role challenge.

As the chief of the trauma center and now the command chief's stand-in, there were always times we have combat casualties, and I was intimately involved in these sad events. But one time comes to mind, and it is my best example of the burden of leader positions and how you can be anointed by followers as a leader. Remember: you don't get to appoint yourself a leader; your subordinates do that.

We were doing the vice president's visit at the same time we had a couple of Air Force warriors get wounded and killed. One was a bomb tech—he had been blown up and lost a leg. I won't put his name here, but let's call him Staff Sergeant Jones. We rallied to his needs and did all the things we do for our warriors. As that started to settle down, I got a call saying that Staff Sergeant Jones was killed in a helicopter crash. I said, "No, he lost his leg; I just talked with him." They said no, it was a different Staff Sergeant Jones (they had the same rank and first and last names).

Once we cleared this coincidence and started to deal with the grief of another lost airman, we had to plan. These events drove a few things, one of which was a brief, respectful memorial for the individual and some services on base. Unfortunately, we were well practiced in this and had a process and strategies on how to best handle all of these casualties.

This one was different. We were conducting airfield operations in support of the ground troops, and we had day-to-day operations on schedules. This had to fit into all that so we could avoid disrupting the battle rhythm. In combat, tough calls need to be made, and leaders do that. Not everyone is happy, but it is acceptance of that burden that your followers watch for and need from a person in a leadership role.

I wish this was fiction, but it was very real. As the stand-in command chief, I sat on the senior team working on the logistics of this and as an adviser to our one-star general who ran the wing. He was the person in the leadership position; he had the tough job here every day.

The planning started, and we decided on a time of day for the event. Here it all went sideways. You see, the Staff Sergeant Jones who was killed in action was Jewish. For Jewish people, you don't have services of this type until after sundown. We had operations to support late in the day and could not make that happen. One member of our advising team was our chaplain. He was doing his job well and advocated for moving everything to meet this religious ritual.

Needless to say, it was tense in the room, and everyone spoke up. We had thousands of soldiers to support that evening and night and had to take all of it into consideration. Then all eyes were on this general, and he firmly explained all the factors in the decision and decided we were having the ceremony as scheduled. It drove some anxiety, sadness, and anger, and he may have lost a few followers, but he acted. He made a decision nobody else wanted to make, and he gathered us up and pulled us together, and that chaplain put on one of the most moving ceremonies I have been a part of.

You see, this old chief anointed that general in my eyes at that moment as a leader. This general and I went through a few more dicey events, and I found him to be one of the best.

LESSONS FROM ARE LEADERS BORN THAT WAY?

- If you are in a leadership role, make the tough calls, but bring your people along.
- Just because someone is first to the feed truck doesn't make them the leader.
- Who are your leaders? Find them. Often, they are not the CEO or sitting in the corner office.
- Why, who, or what are you following?
- Are you leading or yelling or telling? They are not the same.
- Leaders explain their decisions. Do you?

Aspire, Don't Desire

Saddam Hussein's Chair in Baghdad

Farmers are fun to listen to. They always wish they had another hundred acres, a hundred more head of whatever they are raising, or a new tractor. They always want lower fertilizer prices and higher prices for their products. I find it motivating because they don't desire it or take shortcuts to achieve it. They aspire to get there, make a plan, and work at it daily to someday have all that and more. Farmers aspire to grow the best and feed the world. They put that responsibility on themselves, and they work.

There's no alternative to working hard, and the paths to what you aspire to be are sometimes difficult and require persistence. I learned from some of my Air Force brothers and sisters a way to get to a place in life that made me ill. It was driven by desire, wanting to have a title or be in a power position, a place that offered privilege. I watched people dress differently, smoke cigars only to stop later, and lose incredible amounts of weight only to gain it back immediately after not getting a job they wanted. I saw them wanting to be something and not wanting to do the work for it. They desired but stopped aspiring.

That never works on the farm. Shortcuts make you broke, such as buying a new tractor so people think you are doing well. They can make you ill or end your career if you take legal or other shortcuts. I often felt like a salmon. I swam against the current a lot, sometimes because I didn't know better and sometimes because I aspired to be in a position that gave me the ability to advocate and change things to make people more effective and better. I am surprised I got as far as I did in the Air Force because of those who came up with me through the ranks, some making it to the top, sold out on their values and sometimes their morals.

Not until I retired did I think back on this and realize I sleep pretty well at night. Was I perfect? Far from it. Was I doing my best? I know I was, but was I honest and true to myself until the day I left? Absolutely. I may have strayed at times, but not for long.

I remember these examples in my military time, and boy, they stick out worse in the civilian world. A couple of small examples set up some lessons that are woven into this life of mine.

Most recently, I was an emergency manager for a healthcare region, three hospitals and thirty-some clinics. This required me to help prepare these places for events like mass casualties. (I am an emergency manager, among other things). Another job was to prepare for a pandemic. I had thought our country was at risk for such an occurrence and decided we needed an exercise and some discussion. So we did an exercise as a community. This was about four months before we knew anything about Covid. Then the real thing happened. We had some plans done, had a great infectious diseases doctor, and were trying to get the organization to a place where we could handle what was to come.

Then it happened all over again. Those with titles, who embraced corporate values like deference to expertise, decided they had all the answers, marginalized the experts, and pushed us aside. You see, these people looked at a tragedy as a chance to advance themselves, the need to have their face on things. It was nauseating, and I had to make a decision, so I left the organization and moved to another area where I could be helpful during Covid.

I also always remember being at a function with fellow chiefs. We all had big titles and lots of responsibility. We all had taken a path to our roles differently, but you could feel the desire in the room from people who used to aspire. As one of the chiefs came in a bit late, he said out loud, "You all have your shirts tucked in; I have mine out," and he tucked his shirt in. Hey, man, leave it out; be yourself.

There are many lessons in this. If you have been one of these people, or even stepped on it occasionally, I hope this makes you think a bit. I sleep well at night because I was consistent with being the best I could be. People may say differently or call me out about a moment in time, but this farm kid finished his race as a farm kid, aspiring to places where I could make the greater good better and not to be in a place of privilege. I sleep well.

LESSONS FROM ASPIRE, DON'T DESIRE

- Be real to yourself and your followers.
- When it is lonely, it doesn't mean you are in the wrong spot.
- If you desire something, do the work. Shortcuts are dangerous and at times dishonest.
- Protect your integrity.
- You are special. Let people see that. If they judge you negatively, move on.
- Surrounding yourself with mediocrity breeds mediocrity. Hang out with "farmers."

Make the Tough Call

Handing out awards and recognition - the best part of the job!

This chapter will be a bit tough to write. It reminds me of a lonely time when I really had to make a tough call and stick by it. The farm continuously presents you with decision points. Do I go or not? Do I plant or not? Do I sell or not? In some cases, you have to decide to put an animal down, even your best dog. Usually, there is no board meeting to make these decisions. You are on your own with your tools and experiences and courage.

As I rose through the ranks and became responsible for people and programs, I found that you normally had choices on ways to proceed. The decisions are always the same: Is it moral? Is it ethical? Is it legal? Once you pass these hurdles, then you usually have procedures and processes to help you. Then you make the call. I often wanted to make the easy call to keep everyone calm and happy. It is easy, lets you move on to the next challenge, and take it off your to-do list.

The other way is more difficult. It may require change, it may require an unpopular course or path, it may require moving people into different jobs—and it may require you to put it all on the line and do what is right. And doing what is right can be lonely. I have a few of these stories, but this next painful story best leads to lessons learned and tough calls made.

I was stationed on a Turkish base with over one hundred Americans for a nuclear mission. It also happened to be during Desert Storm and the Iraqi invasion of Kuwait. We had some restrictions, as you can imagine during this time, and my position in the unit was one of only two medical personnel. We were both advanced medics and ran our own clinic. We tested water, tested food, put in temporary fillings, and ran our own pharmacy. Most of the personnel didn't know our names, we were just Doc.

On Christmas Eve of that year, a young airman told me he was having trouble urinating and needed me to see him. So, in my ugly sweater, I took him to the clinic (aid station) and examined him, took a sample, and did a lab test. I knew he had an infection and needed an IV and antibiotics. At this point, we were required to call an MD. Air Force doctors were sometimes in other countries or hundreds of miles away. We discussed the case and the treatment, and the MD or PA would authorize the use of narcotics or antibiotics as a cosignatory.

I called the doctor and reported out, and it was fairly routine. However, the doctor wanted me to send the patient to where he was the day after Christmas and let him check on him for a few days. This wasn't common but not unusual for these types of diagnosis. To better set the stage, there were three doctors at this location, two younger docs and one senior officer who commanded the unit. He was a doctor and a colonel and had been in the Air Force for a long time. On this night, I called the colonel, as he was on call. I started treating my patient and sent him to this other location to see the doctor and get further evaluation. After a week, he returned feeling much better and stopped in to say thank you.

The next day, my world changed. Being the "doc" is a great job, and you have access to a lot of people, and relationships are special. I had a great relationship with my doctors at the other location, especially the two younger docs, but that relationship and others were about to be strained. I was about to be tested like a farmer during a drought, or worse.

That young airman and his supervisor grabbed me, as they had a concern. Apparently, there were some examinations during his stay that seemed unorthodox to them. The young airman described these to me, and they were nothing I had ever heard of in my time in medicine. Not only did they seem odd; they seemed to be a form of sexual assault. I made sure the airman had the support he needed and then sealed his records.

We had a law enforcement master sergeant on our site, and I called him and let him know what my concerns were. Once you do this, the wheels of military investigation and justice start to turn, and there is no going back. I spent a short time thinking, *If I say nothing, it will just go away.* I didn't dwell on it, but it did cross my mind.

What I didn't know what was coming was a very lonely existence for about six months. As the investigation began, people had to be interviewed, and once the interviews were conducted, they all knew I was the whistleblower, the snitch, the idiot, the young guy who didn't understand. People turned on me, and my relationships became difficult, distant, or hostile. Everyone loved this colonel, and who was I, a lowly staff sergeant, calling him out like this.

My low of lows hit when my favorite young doc really got personal with me in a way, telling me I didn't understand what it takes to be a doctor or what I was messing with and basically said I should watch my back. My phone calls and referrals became hyper-scrutinized and tense. I was afraid to call or refer, and they had no use for me. I was lonely. I had some support, but it was from those closer to my airman who had the issues, and I had a lot of conversations with myself that said, *I wish I hadn't said anything*, but I knew that wasn't true. I needed to make this tough call.

This atmosphere and stress continued for four or five months until one day the investigator called me to let me know that they'd had a breakthrough with the case. Apparently, this colonel had been committing similar acts with the wives of airmen and other airmen, both male and female, and they were all coming forward. Years of sexual assaults came out in the open. He said it was a good thing I had reported my suspicions. I said, "Do you know the cost I paid for this?"

He said, "You making the tough call has stopped years of abuse." I am sure you can guess there were also others in my professional environment that knew or suspected but took the easy way out and didn't report. The colonel was prosecuted, served jail time, and lost his career and medical license. A small blurb in *Stars and Stripes* said a medic initially reported it. Those people who were hard on me and judgmental never apologized. Instead, they avoided me for a different reason (I'll assume embarrassment), and those relationships never recovered. This one spot in time in my life frequently crosses my mind when I have to make a tough call. It makes the next tough call easier.

LESSON FROM MAKE THE TOUGH CALL

- The right call is not always the easy call.
- The lonely side is often the right side.
- When everyone is beating on you based on the call you made, that may mean it was the right call.
- If you need help to make a tough call, get it. Find the right help and use it.
- Have no regrets. If you think you may have regrets, you probably will.

A War Story from Iraq

Hero's Highway

I woke up today watching TV and seeing the events unfold in Ukraine. I could smell it all—the plastic explosives, the gunpowder smell, the dank air that hangs over combat areas, sometimes human waste—and in my case, all of it was wrapped in the metallic smell of blood. I watched a video that the Ukrainians insisted the Russians see. It threw me into what we call a deep trigger; it was a place that I had been, smelled, seen, and heard. The cries of the mothers, the pain of the staff, the helplessness that goes with being highly trained and being unable to bring back a small young life to the world and its loved ones. During my time in Iraq, twelve percent of all the cases that came in on helicopters and by road were children. Innocents in life, helpless to defend themselves, became victims of man's inhumanity to man.

Flash back to the farm. On the farm, things die, sometimes because they go to slaughter and sometimes because they are eaten by predators or don't survive trauma or illness. The farm has an ecosystem, and it was something that helped me prepare for life in ways I would never know. In Iraq, as the wartime ecosystem droned on, I was the chief. One of the responsibilities I felt fell to me, was keeping our crisis environment stable. After I had been with my medics for a couple of weeks, they would page me to the trauma bay when things were getting lively. I first thought they needed a spare set of hands, but they never needed that. They were too good, and I was in awe of them as medics and trauma teams. What they needed was someone to lead, have their backs, and lend presence and reaffirmation. So I showed up, and usually worked anyway, and most of the time it required little if anything special. Most of the time.

I saw one of the most amazing things my first or second week there. I was still getting used to this hardened team of medics, trying to see how I could make every aspect of their lives in the wartime environment better, seeing that they were supplied and rested, etc.

One day, the call went out for major trauma. It's amazing to watch the crew respond, much more like people finding their place to sit in church than running to a fire or fleeing a mass shooting: orderly, professional, well-rehearsed, and impressive. I took my normal position, which was to report to the master sergeant and say, "How can I help?" On this day, he said to take my own bed. They were numbered, and bed one gets the worst wounded all the way to eleven or twelve. I was told to take bed five with a couple of other medics. As the casualties rolled in, I was in a great place to see this team work. The smells and the amount of blood can be overwhelming, but there was no yelling, no screaming, not even from the wounded. It was like a silent movie.

And then I heard a very young airman in a natural voice say, "Who is missing a leg?" He repeated this a couple of times until we all looked at the legs of our patients and married up the leg he was holding to the soldier who had lost it. I was floored by this. He was the most professional and trained person in the bunch at that moment, and the least experienced, first combat tour airman we had. It made me realize what I needed to be doing for them as a leader: give presence and support, walk the walk with them every day, and have their backs.

This played out in a way that will forever haunt me, but it was my burden. On more than one occasion, the enemy blew up a city center with suicide bombs using cars or themselves as the delivery system. These days were especially busy and trying. The ambulances poured in, the helicopters showed up, and the majority of the victims were women and children. As before, the page went out, "Chief to the trauma bay." I already knew of the event and figured we were in for a rough day. As I started down the ramp that went from my office into the trauma bay, I could hear the sounds of tragedy and life-changing events. We were well staffed, and the best trained in the world.

I reported in to the shift leader and was told all beds were manned and to just be available. I had the macro view. I could see the entire rhythm of the team. It was ballet in action, and I was proud of the young medics ("medics" includes doctors, nurses, and technicians). As my eyes fell on the room, I noticed we started to get more children than usual, some with minor injuries, others hurt extremely badly. We had one area specifically set aside for major pediatric trauma, and it was full. A child four or five years old lay on the gurney, and he had a lot of people milling around, working hard to bring this young boy back. All the beds were full, and many needed immediate help. Some went straight to operating rooms, but this boy had drawn a lot of manpower, resources that were needed elsewhere. As I assessed the situation, I knew we needed to change our posture.

I went to the bedside and looked at the boy, looked at the interventions, and quickly took note of the manpower being used to save him. Sadly, years of experience told me he wasn't going to make it; his color, his injuries, and the lifelessness I had seen too many times in my life showed me the reality that the team hadn't yet realized. I paused for a moment and moved to the head of the bed. The doctor was giving orders, managing an unstable airway on the boy, and hyper focused. I softly put my hand on his shoulder and leaned into his ear. I said, "Doc, I need you to look up for a second. There is a lot going on here, and we need to consider moving on to the rest of the trauma victims. We are using too many resources here."

The doc looked up, took in the rest of the room, and quickly looked me straight in the eye. He then stood and said, "Team, we need to decide quickly whether we continue or move on to these other victims." We quickly took a poll (not unusual in these events), and the team knew they needed to move on. In a very quick moment, one medic was left with the boy to handle his postmortem needs, and the rest of the team dispersed. We handled over forty trauma victims that morning. We had an impressive survival rate, not 100 percent but darn close.

To this day, it plays over and over again in my head: was it right, was it timely, did others benefit? There are many lessons to be learned from these events. Some of them later helped me make some tough decisions and handle future challenges that were less intense but just as important.

LESSONS FROM A WAR STORY IN IRAQ

- Pull away from difficult situations long enough to look at the bigger picture.
- If you are the leader, then lead; don't get caught watching.
- There are decisions that require the benefit of the greater good.
- If your job is to have someone's back, you'd better be there. They don't check their own six; they count on you to do it.

Appetites Can Kill You

A night out on leave...I survived!

This chapter is not about being fat; it is about your consumption and how that can affect your health, emotional stability, and relationships.

On the dairy farm, when calves are coming off Mommy after being born, you can supplement their milk with powdered milk. I used to love watching and helping with that chore. The calves love to suck, and we would spend hours letting them suck on our hands, a sensation like no others. The calves loved the powdered milk and would gorge through a bottle in no time. I assure you if you kept making bottles, they would drink them all.

Powdered milk has a deep, rich, earthy, creamy smell to it. When you open the bag, it looks like anything powdered you would reconstitute, but I'd be lying if I didn't say it tasted good. Sticking a wet finger in the powder and licking it never happened. (Yeah, right.) Anyway, the stuff is good. Often, I would lick a finger and had a taste; it's like a rich milkshake. On this day, I decided I wanted more than that, so I repeated it a few times. Being a generous guy, how could I leave out these calves? They loved it too, and heck, I didn't have anything else going on. *Let's party!*

I got my hand wet, took it to the calves, let them suck it clean, and repeated that over and over. What was yummy soon became excess, and we were happy and feeling full. I was happy. I knew the calves loved me more than anyone on the farm, and I had done a good thing.

Early the next day, the calves and I both started showing symptoms of what happens when you eat too much dairy product. For me, this was manageable but required bathroom proximity. However, the calves couldn't hide it so well, and if you have ever seen calf scours (diarrhea), you can't miss it, and neither did the farmers. I had to fess up and tell on myself so we knew how to get the calves feeling better. I had actually hurt them with my generosity and lack of control over our appetites.

This leads to personal lessons and some battlefield stories—tough ones, but relevant to this book and what it is meant to share. We all enjoy things, and most of us enjoy things that medicate us—coffee, food, alcohol, drugs, religion, sex, or sports activities. We all choose something, and how we consume it matters.

On a nice June morning, I woke from a long night of celebration with my youngest son. He was on his way to an exciting new job, and I was taking him to the airport. We had a nice chat on the way there, followed by the big hug and "Be safe, son. I love you!" at the curb. He was going to live his dream, and I was feeling great about it. So home I went, but I needed to get some water in me, after partying for real last night.

When I got home, I decided to do some computer work and was in the office for three or four hours. My wife asked me a question, and I stood up to go into the living room. And then it hit me. It felt like my world was going to end. My heart rate went through the roof, I couldn't breathe, and I thought I was going to pass out. Remember, I'm an ER nurse, so we sometimes know too much. My mind went to, *Oh my, I need help.* My wife, the good nurse, took my blood pressure. It was not good, and my fingernail beds were turning blue. My nursing assessment at that time was, *I am dying right now!*

We jumped in the car because I didn't think there was time to wait for an ambulance. My goal for the duration of the drive was to stay alive long enough to get to the ER. We got to the ER, and it almost killed me to get to the check-in desk. This was bad. I was taken back quickly, and it did not take long to discover my problem. I had a blood clot that ran from my groin to my ankle. It had broken loose and sent multiple clots to both my lungs, one of which should have killed me. I got lucky, and boy, did I get some quality time to reflect: *How did I get here?* What's this gift of a second chance?

Let's roll back to the farm again. I come from a family with a culture of drinking. My first real drunk was when I was four years old, and my grandfather thought a little wine was fine for me to have. (That is an ugly, entertaining story for another time.) I was around it all the time: drinking, smoking, and laughing, and people working hard and having fun. We stole a few beers out of the shop fridge, and all of us drank underage.

I enjoyed alcohol. I became a professional user of alcohol. Heck, I could even keep up with the Irish on a trip I took once, and they gave me a gold medal. I used alcohol at times the way I ate powdered milk, sometimes for pleasure and a lot of times to excess. In some ways, it was a sign of manhood or a crazy macho thing. I could go long stretches without it. Deployments where no alcohol was available were no problem, sometimes for up to a year. But when it was around, I used it to excess. I didn't moderate, and I love booze. It is your best friend, never lets you down, is always giving you what you need, and doesn't judge you. It can be such a good friend that you'll change your routine and priorities for it and make dates to go out with your favorite drink.

Here I sat in a hospital room, 247 pounds (heaviest ever in my life by far). I had stopped exercising the way I had all those years in the military, and I had become *really* good friends with booze. I had more time to spend with it now. My relationship with booze was strong, and I relied on it a lot. How could I break up with booze, and to a lesser extent, tobacco? (I liked to chew occasionally.) This was a "friend" I couldn't leave or live without—right?

Just as we beg abused wives and people in environments of mistreatment to leave, get away, and find a new friend, which is hard and has a high recidivism rate, I was at that crossroads. I had to take a love in my life and divorce it, walk away from it, and leave it in the past as a memory and a reminder of what could have been and what the future would be without that friend in my life. I was a fun guy when drinking, hilarious at a party, smarter, and could hold court. (I talk too much as it is.)

So what happened to me? That day with my son was the last day I had a drink of any kind. I divorced my love, realized it wasn't my friend, and started life without it. What I quickly realized, now that I had a clear head, was that I wasn't so funny. In fact, there were times it could have cost me my marriage and my career and maybe landed me in jail. I found that I was not doing or enjoying the things I loved unless I drank, and I needed to be around people who understood this, respected me, and were helpful for my post-divorce life. Piece of cake, right? Absolutely not. There are still days when I crave a drink or start to build a plan to have a drink. It is not easy; the love of so many years still comes calling. Quitting has been a blessing and one of my greatest accomplishments in life, and I pray daily that I have the continued strength to stay sober for the rest of my life.

As I divorced certain things in my life, it opened a door to some new friendships that have been true blessings, and certainly make me believe that we end up in places that are blessings. As I was working through the early days of this divorce, I met a now dear friend. She was working on Covid issues with me, and we talked about ourselves and shared stories. My friend had lost her mother suddenly, her father to suicide, and her husband to sudden death—all in the span of a couple dozen months. She had endured extreme loss, and as we talked through each of these, she shared more of how she lost her husband.

The weight of this story and her continued friendship have made me stronger every day, and I realize I need to use my extension of time on this earth to give back. You see, her husband had a relationship with another love in his life, the same one as I did. He had some of the same challenges and struggles, but the difference was that he didn't get to survive his catastrophic event. He was lost to her at a very young age, and when that happens, it leaves many unanswered questions. I see how when someone goes suddenly, whether by suicide or sudden death, those left behind ask themselves a lot of questions about how they might have done something differently and worry that they may be partially to blame.

We all have these types of burdens, and I am so thankful to my dear friend. We have answered a lot of questions for each other, and she has helped me realize that the decisions I have made are the right ones. She pulls me through times when I struggle.

As I mentor younger people, I talk about these challenges with these bright-eyed aspiring folks. I hope it helps all of them, but if it saves just one, then I gauge that as a victory.

Things I have realized about my drinking days: I could have hurt someone badly, emotionally, and physically. If I did and know it, I need to make that right. I could have derailed a career that gave as much to me as I gave to it. I made some mistakes along the way that

I am not proud of. We all have those, drinking or not, but I wish I'd had fewer of them, and boy, did I waste a fortune on that love of my life. The money spent on drinking and tobacco is scary to think about, and what I could have done with all that cash

LESSONS FROM APPETITES CAN KILL YOU

- Keep yourself in a good place with the ones closest to you. You never know when it all can come to an end.
- If you think it's excessive, it is…duh!
- If you know you need to move on from something, then get help and move on. Don't wait for a near-death experience to make it happen.
- Listen to your true friends. You know their message comes from love.
- You don't have to do things like drink to fit in or be cool or have friends. Lead yourself. Don't follow others to a bad place.
- Have the courage to move on from bad habits and situations. There is a bright side beyond the present. Just get started.

Attitude and Max Fab

The Max Fab Flag

I've watched a lot of farmers over the years talk about adversity, challenges, and what the future might hold. Sometimes the outlook sounded bleak or daunting. Things like dry weather or drought, disease in a crop or a herd, or the price of grain or hay—it all can mount up and be crippling. The same is true in military operations. You can have long boring times away from family, you can have days like I've described in previous chapters, and you can get pretty down and lonely. The good news is there is a cure.

When I was rotating out of Iraq, the team threw together a quick go-away for me. It was a bit more than I deserved, but one gesture stood out to me as a validation of at least one small thing I got right.

My daily routine consisted of a lot of push-ups (I hate push-ups) with the troops going off duty and coming on. It was my way to check on them, get their needs, look them in the eye, and sometimes steal a phone from their hands and talk with their moms or dads (special teary-eyed talks, but so fulfilling). Regardless, we all did push-ups. By the time I was done, it was usually 120 to 150 push-ups, depending on who I ran into. As I did these buddy checks, I was always asked, "Chief, how are you doing?" My response was always "Maximum fabulous."

There were a couple of items at the trauma center in Iraq that were unique. Some are now in the museums that surround our capitol in Washington, DC. One article is a large American flag (there were five or six total throughout the Iraq war) that was draped inside the small, covered tunnel known as Hero's Highway that led from the helicopter medical evac pad to the trauma bay. These flags were huge, and each of them has been preserved for history. We all would love to have one of those.

When my commander asked what I would like when I left, I said, "The medical red cross/red crescent flag that flew over the trauma center." He smiled and pointed out that those were hard to get. I knew this, but hey, you can ask, right?

Well, the day came, the going-away happened, and the commander sang karaoke. (He is one of the finest leaders I have ever been around but less of a singer.) He shared some kind words, and they will never be far from my thoughts. He was amazing. When he stood up to say a few words, he presented me with the flag. It was a white flag that wasn't so white anymore. It was brownish from its time flying over our heads. Along the bottom of the flag, in bright red stitching, were these words: *maximum fabulous!*

To this day, that flag makes me think. It hangs where I can see it every day when I park in my garage, and it reminds me of the one thing I need to maintain every day—my attitude. You see, a lot of things are out of our control. As badly as we want something to be easier, better, or more of or less of, we can't control them. The one thing you can bring to bear each day is an attitude, a good, consistent attitude that is positive and breeds an infectious atmosphere within your close relationships and with people you lead.

Max Fab, as I shortened it to, became the rally cry during tough times, when we were lonely, tired, scared, or trying to deal with the difficult sights and sounds of a war zone trauma center. It was imperative that every day I brought my best: my best effort, my best physical and mental state, and my best attitude. I was like a virus. I was contagious, and I needed to control what I was spreading. I chose to spread *Max Fab*. It was the top of the food chain as far as attitude, and our team deserved nothing less.

I could have done a lot of things better during this time and throughout my career, but I know that when my attitude was *Max Fab*, it made everyone around me better, and that was what I could control all the time every day. The times *Max Fab* wasn't there bred the type of reactions you can imagine.

So make the choice, take it on, and challenge yourself. Present yourself as *Max Fab* and change your family and the organizations that are lucky enough to have you! Those farmers I watched working so hard were *Max Fab*. They always had hope, and they were great role models.

LESSONS FROM ATTITUDE AND MAX FAB

- Shed the burden of worry about things you don't control.
- Shed energy on attitude development and control.
- Look for the opportunities in adversity. Highlight them and make them *Max Fab*.
- Enthusiasm breeds enthusiasm.
- You own your attitude and how people perceive it. Be a good steward.

Don't Take Yourself Too Seriously

Hero's Highway in Balad, Iraq

People who know me would say I have a sense of humor. Some love it, and some probably don't appreciate it. I can be a handful for sure, and it is all out of joy and fun and trying my best to keep it light. How do I know this? Well, the people in life who know me best are the kids I grew up with, and when it came time to hand out recognition before high school graduation, they anointed me, not a leader, but a class clown.

How does that apply to the farm? You'd better learn to laugh, because sometimes it helps you work through the rough spots. When something crazy happens—a truck breaks or you slip in the barn and fall into cow shit—you immediately have a choice: let it ruin your day or have some fun with it. We farm kids have all fallen in cow shit, and somebody is laughing.

It took some special people in my career to get me to stop taking myself so seriously. (My wife would tell you I still need work.)

We push ourselves hard to provide for a family, be successful, and reach goals. We run the risk of taking ourselves too seriously. The danger in this is you actually digress in what you are trying to achieve. People around you are the first to know when you take yourself too seriously. It sounds like this. "Dude, lighten up. It's all good. Relax." We have all said it and heard it, and it causes anxiety in some people.

This is the part where you are thinking, *But I can't help it, Dave.* I smiled when I wrote that because I felt the same way. How can anyone keep their edge if they aren't serious about it?

One year, I was at a battlefield nursing course in Texas. We had a mix of fun people in our class, and it was an intense trauma course that required some skills and hard work. I was there as myself (the class clown), so the rest of the team thought they would make me the center of some detailed fun. One night the class was going out, and I went to visit a friend. Unbeknownst to me, they had plans. This clever bunch talked the hotel clerk into letting them into my room. They took a few personal things, moved things around, and redecorated my room and bathroom. It was a well-deserved prank toward a joker and a fun-loving guy. The appropriate thing would have been to say, "You got me," have a good laugh, and use that for what it was: a bonding moment. After all, it was a show of love, as they took time to spend it on me. That is not what happened.

I took it wrong. Far from laughing, I called the cops. The cops came. The clerk got in trouble, and the class all got talked to officially back on base. It was a total disaster because I took myself way too seriously, reacted in a way that was destructive, and destroyed some relationships. I like to think I am better today, but I think we are all victims of our pace in life and are continually vulnerable to taking ourselves way too seriously. I regret that event, but as I said, lessons are to be learned from the good, the bad, and the ugly.

On the flip side, years later, when I was a brand-new chief and stationed in North Dakota, I was walking with a couple of young sergeants across the base. It was the dead of winter and icy. As we were walking, I slipped and hit so hard on my back and elbow that it sounded like a baseball off a bat. It hurt. I was covered in snow, and I had to take a minute to gather myself.

I looked up at these young ladies and sergeants. Here was the chief, down rolling in the snow and ice, and they had tears in their eyes—not from sadness but from sheer, restrained laughter. They could barely ask if I was okay, so I summoned up a big smile, and we laughed pretty hard. (It actually made the pain better.) I gathered myself up, threatened to demote them if they told anyone about it, and joined them in laughter for the rest of the morning. In that one small reaction to adversity, I had developed a relationship with them, and they formed an opinion about how I led and how I handled adversity. Two different outcomes, for sure.

LESSONS FROM DON'T TAKE YOURSELF TOO SERIOUSLY

- Breathe. It's probably not as bad as it first seems.
- Take a ten-second pause. It may save a lifetime of relationships.
- Don't take yourself so seriously that it keeps you from getting where you want to be.
- Laughter is healthy. When you fall in shit, have a chuckle. Others are going to, regardless.

Teach to Learn, Learn to Teach

Rodeo in Wyoming

This is not a chapter about teachers in the literal sense. This is about teaching and a lost part of leadership and self-development. On the farm, there is always that something that comes around once in a lifetime. A large irrigation pipe breaks, or the barn roof flies off. Those are moments when maybe only one or two people have seen and have fixed or know how to fix it. These people are teachers. They show you how to get it done and pass that knowledge along.

It always amazed me to watch people work hard to build admirable careers, and then stop teaching—almost as if they were scared that the knowledge shared would somehow make them weaker. The cliché is true: knowledge is power.

I once had coffee with a friend, someone I mentor. She is very bright and very introverted, so we are 180-degree opposites. She is also a true cowgirl, with a background in rodeo, and she married a man who's the same. She has two awesome kids, and they both rodeo as well. They are very good and win all kinds of awards and sometimes money. They have championship saddles and buckles, and they can fill a room with them.

Her twelve-year-old daughter competed nationally this year and is by far the best rodeo cowgirl in our area. This is a blessing and a curse. There are cowgirls chasing her in competition, and this, as you can imagine, causes situations at school and in social environments that are relentless among twelve-year-olds. Some of the guys pick on her, probably because she is a winner. What these girls don't see is the time and effort she puts in to be that good. She has become the holder of the knowledge and expertise—the barn builder.

As we were talking about her challenges with these girls, I suggested having her teach. She could invite the girls to the ranch, have them train with her and teach them, and start sharing some of her gifts. I argued that teaching would make her better, showing what she's learned, and reteaching herself at the same time. The outcome of these fixes the social problem and gives a few young women an opportunity to grow.

As I mentioned before, I had leaders who reached extreme heights where I never felt they should be. They were turtles balanced on a fencepost. You don't know how they got there, you know they didn't get there by themselves, and if somebody doesn't help them down, they will perish. It would make all the sense in the world when these people, working on hard problems and getting tough questions, would say, "Well, what you didn't know…," and then give you a lot of data that you should have had, could have had, and should have been taught and shared. These people made themselves smaller and were not anointed as leaders.

The gifts we are given as we walk through life, love, and leadership are meant to be regifted. They are not exclusive to any of us, and I believe that we have a responsibility to pass this along, hence this book. We need to teach. You don't need a PhD to teach; you need a PhD in life, experience, or a trade to be able to teach. When you share, you make yourself stronger, and you transmit respect and inclusion to those you lead or look up to. You get stronger and smarter, and once you turn loose the concept that "they don't need to know that" and instead, teach and share, you'll find people become more creative, more loyal, and safer and more efficient. You build through sharing knowledge. I never saw an organization crumble because they shared and taught. Frankly, I have seen the opposite.

I was asked to be the incident commander for an institution during Covid response. This institution was filled with highly intelligent people yet were novices in command, control, and leadership. They were almost completely devoid of true leaders. When I first formed the team to tackle all the challenges Covid was bringing, I immediately started teaching—teaching them my tools, my strategies, how the processes worked, what each position was responsible for, and how to execute. Most of them were attentive and receptive and willing, and it was a pleasure to work with these people—up to a certain point. One of the tenets of crisis management is communications. Most people think this is a news report or press release. This is where I saw the "teach to learn" and "share to be stronger" ideals discounted.

We had decided to start town halls, which were weekly updates with questions and answers. We assembled subject matter experts, and we briefed on everything that we could that was factual. We adjusted to calls for certain data and cautioned on areas that were best guesses at the time, but we still shared and taught. This became our most effective tool, and to this day, continues to be in all crisis situations.

In this case, it was the first thing the senior leaders wanted to do away with. They saw no value in it and felt the organization didn't need to know "all that stuff." At that moment, they made themselves smaller. They didn't want questions because new ideas or things we hadn't thought about were looked at as a hindrance instead of making the team stronger. Some of these people, who were in positions that required them to lead, had labels from that day forward as something much less than a leader. They would never recover from this critical mistake. These were lessons learned the hard way by very educated people.

LESSON FROM TEACH TO LEARN, LEARN TO TEACH

- Your knowledge is power—after you share it.
- Sharing and teaching make the collective *you* stronger.
- Wherever you are in an organization or family, don't let the thin air near the top make you forget about the masses below you. They are watching and you will be anointed appropriately.
- If you are not teaching and sharing, someone is. Is it what you want spoken or taught?
- When people find out that you didn't share and you should have, they disengage.
- Fight for feedback. Get the information you need. Don't be a sheeple.

Every Day is Sunday

After a long day in Turkey - Desert Storm

Now you might be thinking, *What does milking cows have to do with my life?* Here's the thing: We all have to milk the cows. Growing up, I watched a lot of farmers take on the daunting task of committing to the dairy business. This is one of the most admirable and amazing things to be part of. Once you commit, every day is Sunday.

Studies show that, for average people, working a Monday through Friday workweek, their most stressful day of the week is Sunday. Sunday is the day when we worry about tomorrow. We have to get up, go in, and face people and challenges and give our time to things we may not want to. I hope everyone in life finds a great job they love, has coworkers that enrich their lives, and has a balance between work and life that is healthy and fulfilling. If you are one of these people, great. In reality, the odds are you may not be.

I worked on more farms than just dairy. Some grew almonds, grapes, and other harvests. They required long days and not much rest. It requires commitment and persistence. Harvest ends, and there is a lull, just as in most of the work we do—but cows make every day a Sunday. Dairy farmers worry about tomorrow every day. They have to calculate, plan, and prioritize constantly. They work mainly with animals and not people, and the call to action is every day, twice a day. And that's just to milk, not to mention everything else.

My routine on my last combat tour was 6.5 days a week. I would get up at 0330, be out by 0400, do checks and push-ups, get on my knees with our chaplain, and handle what the world threw at us until 2000 or 2100 hours. I never missed getting exercise. I only broke that routine on Sunday, when I slept until I woke, usually 0500, cleaned my living area, did the laundry the best I could, and hit the gym and church. Then it was lunch with my commander and off I went until 2100. This routine was frequently disrupted but helped me work through stress and fatigue. Our cows were constantly being milked.

Once we accept and realize that, whatever life brings, we all have to milk the cows, then we can accept what that takes. What do you need to do to help sustain yourself and maintain balance? The amount of energy we spend on those "Sundays" is wasted. We can build healthy lifestyles and routines, or unfortunately, some choose poor mechanisms such as drinking or other excesses. These don't help and actually make things worse because, in the end, the cows will still be there, needing to be milked.

LESSONS FROM EVERY DAY IS SUNDAY

- Learn to detach from your cows, especially on Sunday. It will all be there on Monday.
- Accept that the cows have to be milked. Do your best to make it fun and enjoyable.
- If you hate milking cows, then find something else to do. The cows deserve better.
- Don't let the cows drive you to drink or worse. Develop healthy habits.
- Make milking a place you enjoy and one that enriches you, no matter what farm you are on.

Slow Down to Go Faster

With my Cousin in Iraq (he's one of my heroes, too)

As we all get older, we have moments we reflect on, saying things to ourselves like *Boy, that was a dumb thing I did* or *What was I thinking?* Hopefully, these are said with a chuckle and a feeling of relief that nothing bad happened. These comments are sometimes made when somebody says, "How did you get that scar?" or "What happened to your leg?"

On the farm, I heard stories about why a fence didn't close right or why there was a dent in a tractor or piece of equipment. The stories oddly had similar tones. The dent or bad fence story would start with something like this: "We were in a hurry because it was going to hail or getting dark or we needed to get to the next chore or make it to town for the big game." It didn't matter if it was a scar on a forehead or a dent in a tractor; they were all reminders of a time when you wished you had slowed down and taken your time. Many of these stories ended with, "We wound up spending more time getting the chore done because we had to fix the fence or go get stitches."

Working across the full spectrum of medical care, I was an EMT, nurse, manager, and executive leader, all multiple times, both medical and civilian. During my early years, we would hear, "Code blue, XYZ room," and ran to get there, arriving winded, weak, and unable to effectively do CPR or administer meds. We had to pause and waste time. Later, we all started to walk. Yes, we got there a few seconds later, but we saved time because we gave ourselves time to think, and we could perform immediately upon arrival. We slowed down to go faster.

As I grew through this profession and my military career, I was an audience to proverbial dented trucks and broken fences. Sometimes, late in my career, it would sound like this: "Chief, go to XYZ base and find out what is going on and help them fix it" I could tell you many stories, but my goal is hopefully to portray an environment you may find yourself in, may be creating, or may have been a victim of.

This phenomenon I call normalizing recklessness. You might call it risky, dangerous, or irresponsible. I call it normalized recklessness because the truck dents and the broken fences are a result of a culture that is driven by the "leader," the person in charge. This may be you or your organization, or it may be a culture driven by a system or the Department of Defense.

I would remind the medics I served with of an odd dynamic: they had two professions to answer the call to, a military and medical profession. We had to meet all the standards of military life and simultaneously meet civilian medical regulations and standards. This is the double whammy of daily pressure to "get in before it hails or rains."

As you ponder these stories, they may sound familiar. In the military, there is a cliché that says if you are not fifteen minutes early, you are fifteen minutes late. That sounds funny, but it is an expectation. Tardiness is frowned on and can lead to discipline. This approach breeds an underlying stress to manage your time, and in the military, it is necessary. On-time is essential to combat operations and to our nation's defense, and to this day, I frown on people who are late. But wait. Is that always healthy? Is it the best way to approach everything? Remember, trying to get to the opening kickoff of the big game might end in a dent or worse.

I worked for an organization that had a large medical footprint and was a large facility in a large region. My position required me to attend what was called a safety huddle. This was a very detailed event, structured by repeated daily reporting of anything that could be a trend or critical safety event that needed to be brought to attention. As I attended these, I noticed a trend, helped by my nursing experience and years of being in positions that required me to lead. Almost daily, someone in the facility had made a medication error.

At this time, my boss was a nurse and in charge of this and also quality for the facility. She was anointed by me as a leader, and we went through some trying times together. As we worked through the "why," we speculated and agreed the fence was broken. As we talked, I told her, "I think we need to slow down to go faster." She said, "What do you mean?"

Being a nurse and a military man, I explained to her the many times I was asked to dissect a root cause of a poor outcome. For example, why did an airman get paralyzed from the neck down in a vehicle accident while going to the field for duty? Why did a critical component to a very critical weapons system get dropped and destroyed, requiring national command authority notification (a super big deal)? I told her they were going too fast. They needed to be on time (remember, in the military "on time" means you're fifteen minutes late), so they were in a hurry, and it cost a young future and a near miss of unbelievable consequence.

These medication errors were being made by highly trained, licensed personnel, altruistic and thoughtful, but they had been subjected to a culture that demanded volume and velocity to better increase a margin in earnings and profits. This required some to work faster, and at times, to take shortcuts.

Does this sound familiar? Are you part of a culture that drives hazardous behaviors or practices, or are you promoting a similar culture? In life, we go fast at everything we do. At times, we say things like, "There are not enough hours in the day" or "I can't get it all done." These are signs that you or your processes are going too fast. There are many examples of what I describe. Some of this ties into the chapter on *Listen*, and some of it ties into self-discipline and culture.

LESSONS FROM SLOW DOWN TO GO FASTER

- If you feel as if you are going too fast, you are. Listen to your inner alarms.
- Pressure and a culture that drives increased speed without proper management will put a dent in your tractor.
- Don't go so fast that you forget to put on your seatbelt in life. It might be the last thing you do.
- Don't go so fast that your loved ones become a blur. If you can't focus on them because of your speed limit, then give yourself a "ticket" and slow down before your kids or significant others do. The dent you get may become a scar.

- The margin or bottom line is never an excuse for someone getting the wrong pill or losing their life. Check your culture and your values, both personal and professional.
- Respect people enough to not require them to speed, and don't speed yourself.
- Can you remember the last time when something awful happened because you didn't speed?

Kids Know Everything

My first official Air Force photo, Basic Training 1984

Fifteen assignments in thirty years took me around the world. One thing it taught me was, if you watch the kids in any culture, they are all the same. They have similar needs and similar parents doing the same parent things, and they are honest and attentive and little sponges. I learned more about culture from watching kids around the world than from adults at times. Enjoy these stories as I talk about being a kid and the "kids" I worked with and for.

I said to a friend the other day, "Kids show us what we need to demonstrate daily to succeed as a people and a human race." I always get a look that says, *Explain that to me*. My explanation includes a joke, a kid story, and a life of experience living in many countries and experiencing many cultures.

First, the joke: What are the three things that never tell a lie? The answer is kids, drunks, and yoga pants.

Next, the kid story: I was pretty observant as a kid and wanted to know things, but for a time, when I got interested in something, I made sure I knew everything there was to know about it. I was on a trip with my mother and grandmother. We had spent a very cool day out that ended in a movie (there were no movie theaters in the nearest town), and we were on our way back to a relative's house. It was late, and we didn't have GPS in 1973. As we were returning, I remembered something I had seen on the way out; it was a flashing construction sign near the house we were staying at.

As my mother was driving back, she turned one street too soon on the way to the house, got caught on a side street, and had to struggle to get back on the right street. No worries, that happens. But this happened *four times!* Between my grandmother and mom, they kept making the same mistake. By the third decision to make the same wrong turn, I was in the back, seven years old, saying, "Keep going straight to the light," to which the response was something to the effect, "Keep it down, be quiet, you are not helpful," and the like. Finally, after these two had exhausted all their efforts, my grandmother said, "Why don't you do it like Dave said and see?" We got to the house in about two minutes, and all was well.

My mother and my grandmother had discounted my contributions to finding our way home because I was just a kid. I wonder how many things in life we miss or roads we follow that are more difficult to travel because somebody who gave us advice on a better way was ignored because of their age or stereotype.

I later applied this lesson through years of leadership in the military, and it served me well. I will tell you, not everyone appreciated me doing what I am about to describe. It made them nervous; sometimes it made them act out in inappropriate ways, and in some cases they got better. The one thing it did for me was make me a better leader, more effective and laser-focused on what I needed to be doing to help support the airmen.

The trick I used (not a trick) was to work at the lowest common denominator. Many times tremendous things happened—not because I was brilliant or special, but because the airmen (kids of the Air Force) armed me with the truth—their feelings and honest challenges.

A few examples from our missile force. When I first started as the command chief at 20th Air Force as the senior leader for all the nuclear missile forces in the United States, I knew I had to close some gaps in my knowledge to best help train, equip, and organize our forces. As I went out, I was always greeted by senior leaders—other chiefs, colonels, officers, and senior enlisted—and I would get the best of the best put in front of me. This force is absolutely awesome and super professional, but I knew they needed things and faced challenges, and most of the bases didn't want to be "bothered" with issues. Hold on! Issues and challenges were my job, so I wanted to talk to the airmen.

So how did I get past all this and get to the real skinny? I went out to the missile field and spent the day and night with them. For those who don't know, the missile field is away from the main base. Most people live at a facility for three days or longer. There are cops, chefs, missileers, and facility managers all out in the vast plains of Wyoming, Colorado, Nebraska, North Dakota, and Montana, 24/7, 365 days a year since the mid-1900s. The best way to hear the "kids" at ground level was to live with them. So off we went, the two-star general and I. We left the main base and received a lot of briefings on all the accomplishments of the wing, hearing high-level needs and a nice dinner out. Then we went to the field, and our days were long.

We would speak to defenders (cops) guarding one missile for twelve hours because the electronic system was down. We went deep underground to chat with our missile officers to see how their world was, but the money was at night. We would pull into a facility, chat with the cook (chefs, actually; they were unbelievable), order something for dinner, have the facility manager brief us and show us to a room, which consisted of bunk beds sleeping six to a room, and then I'd get out of my uniform, put on sweatpants, and go and watch TV, play pool, or work out with the airmen.

On this particular day, we had heard a lot about bad snowmelt, and it had caused problems leaking into the missile silos. We knew there were processes for this to be handled and had been briefed on it. What we didn't know was what the "kids" were seeing, what they thought was a good solution, and how we could help. They saw the flashing construction sign all day, every day. As we sat over breakfast with a couple of very young defenders who had worked all night and were getting ready to go back out, we asked them what we could do for them and what they needed. This is a general and a chief asking questions, so it was not easy for them to be comfy, but they were tired and cold from the night before, and they let us have it a bit.

One of the airmen said, "Chief, I spent all night building a moat." After a chuckle I said, "A moat? Please continue." The airman went on to describe a night where they had reported water intrusion. Remember, these were cops, not engineers. They were told that there weren't resources to help and to start building a diversion for the water with rocks and other earth materials they had. (Turn in your rifle for a shovel, defender.) So as airmen do, they executed this with precision and enthusiasm. (Actually, they were pissed off.)

The general asked where this was, and we were given a location. We both thought it was funny that we didn't get that briefing. So off we went. The general told our captain to drive to the location, and lo and behold, there it was, a finely constructed moat, diverting some water the best way two cops in freezing cold could do in the middle of the night. I know this drives a lot of other questions on leadership and who directed this and why. That was all addressed, but in the end, they didn't listen to the airmen when it mattered or take them seriously.

I had some conversations with our missile maintenance folks about a piece of equipment that was a problem. It had weak areas and broke a lot, and I wanted to get them better stuff. So I employed my strategy and went to the field, talked to the airmen, and reported to the general. This prompted him to have the staff brief him on the status of the equipment. It was to be an all-hands-on-deck from the three main bases all traveling to our location to brief on this issue and other challenges. I had a sneak peek at the briefing, and it didn't portray the message from the airmen. You see, the briefers didn't want to brief the entire detail because of fear they would look bad or not doing their job.

This briefing had omissions, and I shared my concern with the general and asked to bring two airmen from each base to attend the brief. We did that, and I met with them beforehand to ask them to be as truthful with the people in the room as they had been with me.

The meeting started, and the slides were briefed exactly as I had seen them. Once the briefer was done, the general asked if anyone had anything else. When he heard none, I said, "I think some details are missing here, and I have heard differently." The looks all started my way as I said, "General, ask these airmen if that is accurate." Bless these "kids"—they started off by telling the whole truth in front of their commander and senior leaders. It was tense, it was difficult, and I think it saved a life or prevented a serious incident. The people involved are all fine people, working hard at the defense of our nation and focused, but they made a few mistakes along the way. The biggest mistake of them all was not listening to the "kids."

LESSONS FROM KIDS KNOW EVERYTHING

- If someone is screaming, they may be crazy, or they may be telling you something. Investigate.
- Bad news doesn't get better with time. The "kids" have the scoop; go visit them.
- If it looks or seems odd at the top, go to the bottom, and see for yourself.
- Stereotypes and false perceptions are limitations to your growth.
- "Kids" teach up; let them. It's okay. You won't lose anything.
- "Kids" anoint leaders as leaders when they "go to the field." Get your sweatpants on.
- What do your yoga pants say?
- Ask the "kids" this question: Where is the next mishap or accident going to happen? The answer might save a life, a company, or fiscal disaster.
- Leaders are not afraid of "kids."

When You Can't Milk the Cows Anymore

Gramps and the pistol

When I was young, my grandfather was at a point where he wasn't milking every day. He had a heart problem that was always present during my short time on earth with him. The one thing I knew was he was wise, and people frequently sought his counsel and advice. It didn't dawn on me what was going on, but it came full circle when I decided to write this book. My grandfather wanted to pass it along, pay it back, make a difference until the end. He wasn't defined by his physical ability to milk cows or feed animals, and he decided to use the gift of knowledge and experience to teach.

I wrote this book for a couple of reasons. First, I finally heard what people were saying about what I was offering, which was to give back. Second, it has been good for me as I deal with the leftovers of days gone by that will always affect me. Third, for you, whoever you are, I hope, as you have traveled these pages, you found a nugget or two that helps you move along in life a little easier or you offer to help someone along in their lives.

I feel I need to tell a final story for you to ponder as we close this relationship we have built. The story that comes to mind is a story of giving and sums up what a lot of this book is founded on. It is about hard work, taking chances, listening, being a friend, being present, doing for others—I think you get the point—those things that get you anointed as a leader.

Not long ago, I was blessed to run into a high school mate who was a year behind me, and his sister was a year ahead of me. We both live here in Montana and have since started a solid true friendship together, hunting and shooting and weekly coffee. Best of all, we got to work on leading an organization through Covid. While leading the teams during Covid, we would tell stories from home, stories of the farm, and stories of our families.

As we teased out the gaps in our lives from thirty-five years apart, we started to put back together our younger years, and he reminded me of a few things that indirectly shaped me. You see, this book gives back, and I found out and was reminded that it comes from my farm and the people on it who shaped me, and it was to the benefit of those who stood in the combat zone with me and hopefully beyond today and going forward. There is more to tell, but that is for a later time, so I will leave you with this blessed story.

My friend was an orchard farmer mainly, but we all dealt with animals. His farm was four or five miles from my grandfather's, and of course, we were all Catholic and went to church together. It was a small town. How small? When I called my mom to tell her I had run into my buddy, she said, "Did you know your grandfather gave his dad his first loan to start his first orange orchard? He also was unhappy because he paid it off so quickly." You see, my grandfather was always giving, helping, and making a positive difference, and so was my family.

My buddy's older sister was born with special needs and required a lot of attention and physical therapy. These things were not cheap or readily available, so people like my grandmother would build a schedule for ladies of the church to arrive daily to do physical therapy with her. This was a long endeavor for the ladies, and his sister only walks to this day because of them.

This story doesn't surprise me a bit. I saw it come from my grandmother constantly. The giving and improving of her life, her environment, and her community made her family stronger, and we were enriched as she passed those treasures along. It pains me when I see people lose sight of this and stray to a less open giving model in their lives. But we can hope to someday find that time where we all give back, to develop our personal tools and be in a position to pass it along. Everything in this book (and maybe the next) is founded off these basic examples and has stood the test on the battlefield and in my life.

I want to leave you with this. I will never be perfect, and I will never stop trying to be better. I sometimes forget to follow my own words and advice and need help staying grounded, too. I try to make a difference in a positive way every day, and mostly I give. I give of myself, I give of my fortune (I wish I had more), and I will continue to give my best and my all until I pass. Be blessed in all you do, look for your niche, and thank those who need to be thanked, but mostly, believe in you because you are special, no matter what.

LESSONS FROM WHEN YOU CAN'T MILK THE COWS ANYMORE

- Give somebody a loan. It makes you rich in ways beyond money.
- If your "family" needs physical therapy, sign up for the challenge. The result can change a life forever. Be part of it.
- Change your environment for the good; it grows like a weed.
- Giving is getting. Just ask my grandmother or go ask yours or her equivalent.
- Believe in yourself. You are the one person you have to live with for life, so like yourself.
- Your time is valuable. How do you spend it? Is it on the right things? If not, then where should you be spending it?

A Note from the Author

Officially a Command Chief

People write that they're proud of their service. They're proud of being a soldier, an airman, a sailor, or a Marine. I don't see where we transition that sentiment for our veterans as they come out of service. Because you've served proudly, you should be able to live proudly after your service has come to an end, and some things that come along with living after service get lost in translation. During service, during conflict, we go through a lot for our country, and that service means so much to us. We identify with that for a large portion of our lives, and sometimes that service is the pinnacle of our lives.

Along with attachment, belonging, and brotherhood (or sisterhood), we often find ourselves on the wrong end of a mental health crisis. As we transition back to civilian life, we lose part of ourselves, and that's a lot to lose. It includes the moral injury that goes along with the change that comes with making that transition. I'd like people to say, "I'm proud of my service, and I'm proud to be a veteran."

I've learned how to live as a veteran, and that has to be defined so people can get on board with that. We all need to be on board with that, both veterans and civilians. Having conversations with veterans and veteran care providers helps us identify the best way to transition to civilian life, and how to help us live with the injuries and the insults that we have endured. From the physical injuries resulting in frontline combat, to the peripheral injuries that go along with that, or simply just the separation and moral injury from time spent in service, we have to take an active role in supporting that transitional phase. Once we understand that, once we're more involved, then we can get to a point where we can take proactive steps to truly help veterans.

There are common traits among veterans that lead to suicide, homelessness, and substance abuse, and those traits stem from us being able to ask and answer questions about what we can do and why we have the issues we have. Every time I hear or see somebody proclaim, "Proudly served," I wonder if they're proudly a veteran and proudly out in their communities, and if they've been fortunate enough to have found places that continue to honor them for their service by giving them an opportunity to feel like they belong. It's more than just getting what they need in the form of food, housing, and medical care, it's about being able to get *healthy* food, *affordable* housing, and medical care that treats them both *on the outside and the inside*. To those who haven't served but are in our communities that want to help and have professional experience, we need you now.

Remember that the service doesn't stop once we leave the service that we're in. Even when we're done, we still want to be of service. It's ingrained in us. Sometimes, we find those places within our communities, and we can continue to serve as civilians. When veterans are able to do that, it's much easier for people to transition because moving into civilian life is not so dark and daunting. It helps veterans find their purpose in "life after service."

Serving proudly is one thing. Becoming a veteran and being a veteran proudly continuing to serve is another thing, and one we need to address.

Acknowledgments

Whenever anyone takes a leap into the unknown and is a bit vulnerable, there is always somebody who has encouraged, pushed, and influenced them along the way to get to this point. I am no different. I have been super blessed with tremendous people around me to do all those things.

I could list many names here, but I won't. However, for those of you who pick up the phone, send off the text, and reach out for buddy checks—thank you. I need that. To the people in my life who are there on my low days and celebrate my highs—you are true friends.

To all of you I don't know who got to this point in the book with me, I am always up for a cup of coffee or just a quick chat, and I'll be the first to tell you I don't know what I don't know. Otherwise, hold on; you will get all the listening skills I can muster. My family is the best, and they are what keeps me going. I am eternally grateful for their patience and love.

The one thing I always told my boys and continue to do even today is, "Make a difference in some way every day, in a positive way."

Remember: we are all *great!*

Contributions from Darla Tyler-McSherry

A wheat farm in Lonesome Prairie, Montana, is where Darla Tyler-McSherry was raised, leading her to pursue her Bachelor's and Master's degree from the University of Montana in Health and Human Performance. Involved with college health for over 28 years, Darla is the Director of Student Health Services at Montana State University Billings. In addition to her work with the university, Darla serves as the Coordinator for the Yellowstone County DUI Task Force, Treasurer for the Rocky Mountain College Health Association, and Secretary for Horses Spirits Healing.

Darla's passion for helping people inspired her to become the founder and visionary of *Ask In Earnest*, an initiative designed to address mental health, depression, and suicide in the farm and ranch population. She embraces the role of serving as an agent of positive change and advocacy for the farm and ranch communities that helped build America.

About the Author

From a foundation built on growing up in an agricultural environment, Dave Nordel is taking a lifetime of extraordinary experiences and demonstrating the power of "Giving Back!" Grounded in both good and bad, plus over thirty years in the military, Dave harnesses the ability to lead at an executive level and to affect the lives of our nation's sons and daughters, both in peacetime and during conflict.

With forty years of military and civilian leadership, coaching, and mentoring, Dave has transitioned into sharing the gifts he has acquired in the hope of building better leaders, better parents, and better people to close the gaps in our culture, and to enable all of us to improve ourselves through self-development and practicing good mental health.

Dave is a master storyteller and loves to give back through teaching at the collegiate level and in small groups. With a passion for the veteran community, Dave represents the veteran community with a focus on mental health, PTSD, and suicide prevention. He founded Max Fab Consulting with the intention of sharing his talent of writing and speaking, with the hope he can make a difference for people who struggle with the traumas they carry.

An outdoorsman who loves all that has to offer, Dave finds his balance doing the things he is passionate about. He is a board member of Horses Spirits Healing, a non-profit focused on equine therapy to assist veterans and their families with mental and physical health, recovery, and recuperation.

Dave is the proud father of two boys, Dominic and David, and has been married to his wife, Patricia, for over thirty years. He is generous with his time, and mentors aspiring adults to help them achieve their life and career goals. To share the gifts of Dave's experiences and life lessons, visit MaxFabConsulting.com.

An Excerpt from

When the Cows Lie Down

The pressure to not be labeled a "quitter" is something that many of us have experienced at some point in our lives. It can be a powerful force that drives us to do things that we may not want to do, or that may not be in our best interest. But what if quitting is not always a bad thing? What if quitting can be a powerful tool for change and growth?

In her chapter, Darla Tyler-McSherry shares her story of facing incredible adversity and the temptation to give up. But she didn't quit. Instead, she found the strength to keep going, to keep fighting, and to keep believing in herself. Her story is a powerful reminder that quitting is not always a sign of weakness but can be a powerful act of courage and self-preservation.

When the Cows Lie Down delves into the complexities of quitting, exploring the reasons why people quit and the outcomes that can result. From quitting a job to quitting a relationship, the book will explore the various ways that quitting impacts our lives and the lives of those around us.

The book also offers hope and inspiration, highlighting the stories of those who refused to quit and found a way to persevere in the face of incredible challenges. It is a powerful reminder that we all have the strength and resilience to overcome even the most difficult obstacles, and that quitting is not always the answer.

Let us embrace the power of quitting, not as a sign of weakness, but as a tool for growth, change, and empowerment. Learn from Darla's experience, and the stories of others who have faced adversity and emerged stronger for it. And let us never be afraid to quit when necessary, knowing that we have the strength and resilience to navigate whatever challenges life may bring.

Quitting. The word conjures up so many emotions, right? Why do we quit? We do so for many reasons. One is that we quit when we get uncomfortable or unsure or scared of what may be coming next. We can't comfortably predict the future or outcome of our choices and actions, and rather than wade into the unknown, we stay in the known. The choice to remain comfortable can have negative consequences for more than just ourselves.

As a society, we don't deal well with loss and grief. Painful, devastating, life-changing events can propel us into a deep well of darkness, sadness, and despair, and it's not unusual to feel completely alone. My experience with extreme loss confirms this.

It started when I became a member of a club no one ever wishes to join. Ever. I did so when my dad, a lifelong wheat farmer who was born in the same farmhouse my brother and I were raised in, took his own life, right there on the family farm on a warm, gorgeous, Indian-summer September afternoon. We were like so many other members in the club of suicide loss survivors in that we scoured recent events and days searching for answers—answers we will never fully understand while we are on this side of things. Once we completed the perfunctory mechanics involved with selecting flowers, planning the memorial service, ordering food, etc., we were left with an empty, open space to attempt to fill, and navigate moving forward.

Time marched on and I found myself at the two-year mark of my dad's suicide. As the date approached, my husband (Dave) and I were talking about his death. Dave said to me, "You know, I think you're handling this very well. The first year you were in a tailspin."

I agreed. I was handling it well. One factor that made a significant difference for me was getting connected to professional help by working with my medical provider and getting a referral to a mental health counselor who was embedded within the medical practice. The combination of prescription anti-anxiety meds and anti-depressants, coupled with the ability to work with a skilled, trusted professional, helped me address all the emotions that came with being a loss survivor, and allowed me to feel a sense of normalcy, even though now it was a "new normal" for me.

Less than six weeks after having this conversation, and after Dave experienced a brief illness and hospital stay, Dave passed away unexpectedly at home. We thought we had dodged a bullet. Instead, less than sixteen hours after being released from the hospital, the local volunteer ambulance crew, the city/county ambulance service, and the life-flight helicopter all landed at my house within minutes of each another, but to no avail. Dave didn't survive.

Afterward, my mom and I talked about how strange it was to be widows together. It is not the natural order of things. When my dad died, I shared with others that, "I never knew such awfulness could exist," but now I know that it does. With my husband's death, I was introduced to a new level of pain and loss that I never knew existed.

Today, I understand how lucky I am to live in Montana, a frontier state where I am able to walk only ten minutes from my place of employment to my mental health counselor's office. Near the two-year mark of my dad's death, my counselor and I both agreed I was in a good place emotionally and mentally, and that I didn't need to continue sessions. Now, after Dave's passing, I was in my counselor's office twice a week, barely holding on by my fingernails.

I was just getting my feet underneath me for a second time, when my brother called me on Sunday morning in June and said, "I can't get ahold of Mom." I recognized a dull ache in my gut that was telling me that something was wrong, but I pushed on and reasoned that she had gone to church, was still in town, was outside in the garden, etc. That turned out to not be the case. Seven months after my husband passed, my mom was now gone, too.

During this time, what became a profound awareness and extremely visible to me, especially after my husband's passing, is what I called "The 3 Letters" stamped on my forehead. Although all three were interchangeable depending upon the situation, I felt like only one letter at a time was visible to others.

The first letter was a capital "S" for suicide. People often don't know what to say to a loved one left behind, especially after a suicide. So rather than take a risk, be vulnerable, or step out of their comfort zone, people will say nothing. Perhaps in an obtuse way of showing support, some share and discuss myths about suicide with the survivor, not realizing the injury they are causing as the words continue to tumble from their mouths. The survivor with the "S" stamped on their forehead walks alone, even in a crowd. Just being at a social event in a room filled with retired farmers and ranchers left me sobbing, because the "S" throbbing against my head reminded me how similar those men were to my dad.

The second letter stamped on my forehead was a capital "W" for Widow. This was perhaps the most hurtful one. People see it and worry you are contagious, especially if you are a young widow. It is as if other people, especially women, somehow believe that if they talk to you, you might transmit something, and this might cause their husbands to die. I know it was visible to others, for instance, when walking into a social gathering at work. As I approached the room, I could see the quick sideways glances people gave to one another, and I could hear the hushed, "Here she comes" as I entered. I believe the days that the "W" stamped on my forehead were the most excruciating ones. Those were the days that I spent time thinking about whether I wanted to continue to live.

The third letter stamped on my forehead was a capital "D" for Death. These were the days that I didn't feel anything at all. Numbness and emptiness overwhelmed any other emotion. These were the days that I made robotic motions to maintain the most basic level of functioning. I think the capital "D" leaves people feeling invisible. I felt that life was continuing for others, and they could experience joy and happiness and accomplishments. All I could feel were unknown levels of not seeing a future for myself.

During the times when "S" or "W" or "D" were flashing bright and served as a beacon for people to avoid me, I craved even the briefest moments of normalcy. Mercifully, they did appear. Colleagues I didn't know particularly well offered kindness and support by taking me to lunch. Another colleague gave me a pair of mittens she knitted herself. A friend invited me to come to her house on a workday and made lunch for me, which was a huge treat since it was the first home-cooked meal I'd had in weeks. A colleague gave me hugs, and she commended me for "staying upright," even on the darkest of days. My dog, Roo, greeted me with comfort, love, and security every day when I arrived home to my empty house. Most impactfully, a person came into my life through work channels, and as we developed a friendship, I could see that he wasn't afraid of the "S" or "W" or "D." Instead, he accepted me as I was, listened when I talked, and wasn't unnerved by my answers to his questions. He is the truest of friends. He has *given me the best gift. Ever. He has helped me see, and actually experience, that it is okay to live again.*

Regarding quitting, I offer this as advice. Avoid the urge to quit when you encounter uncomfortable or painful situations or conversations. Our simplest gestures can be very important to someone who is hanging on by their fingernails. It doesn't have to be complicated. A cup of coffee, a kind hand-written note, taking the time to sit with the person and just "be" can make all the difference in the world. You don't need to have magical words or advice or solutions because there are none. Quit the guilt of trying to search for them and coming up empty. Your presence, time, and authenticity are what resonate with the person who is hurting. In other words, be willing to quit what might be your "go-to" response by avoiding the hurt and remaining silent and distant. The help you offer to someone may be the difference between warm, healing sunshine and everlasting clouds and cold.

As I write this, I realize I have learned lessons about quitting I wish to pass along to others who are hurting. I want to be sensitive to the situation the reader may find themselves in and make my best effort to not patronize or minimize.

I think it's most important not to quit on yourself. Perhaps unintentionally, I set a marker or a line in the sand that, if I crossed it, would have signaled defeat. For me, I chose getting out of bed every day as my marker. I don't judge others who don't because of their own trauma. However, for me, I told myself that I needed to get out of bed every day. Otherwise, there was no point in continuing. Of course, I took time away from work when these devastating events occurred, but I still got out of bed. There were responsibilities that didn't stop or get put on hold. I still had multiple jobs. My youngest stepdaughter continued to live with me. The pets needed my care and attention. I still had a mortgage to pay. The demands of daily living forced (or allowed) me to place my focus elsewhere, even if for the briefest of periods. I would pull into my parking space at work and put my head on the steering wheel and experience a moment of gratitude for being able to focus on other things for a few hours. Many of these days included tears, inattention, and indifference, but I had gotten out of bed and was doing my best.

My mom had a great saying: "Take things one day at a time, and if that gets too hard, take things one-half day at a time." I've followed this advice on many days, as there were numerous mornings when I woke up and had absolutely no clue how I would make it through the entire day.

Quit the idea that you have to figure it out alone. Talk to your medical provider, get connected with a mental health professional, and recognize and express gratitude for the kind gestures people offer. Quit the fear of vulnerability, and as a result, you may gain a new relationship that has a profoundly positive impact on your life.

In the words of the beloved late Jimmy Valvano, "Don't give up, don't ever give up." You are worth it.

Darla Tyler-McSherry

Stories like these are intended to cover real situations where quitting, including suicide, is an option, where some would say suicide is the ultimate quit. However, when it comes to you, the leader, it is simple. The new generation is values-centered. They not only read and observe your values, they watch you for consistent demonstration of those values, and if those values are misaligned, they leave.

For more information on *When the Cows Lie Down*, follow Dave Nordel at MaxFabConsulting.com.

www.ingramcontent.com/pod-product-compliance
Lightning Source LLC
Chambersburg PA
CBHW050647160426
43194CB00010B/1839